8 STEPS to FINANCIAL FREEDOM

Achieve independence earlier and live life on your own terms

JAMES B. KEEFE

8 Steps to Financial Freedom:
Achieve Independence Earlier and Live Life on Your Own Terms

CONTENTS

To Papa and Dad,
who taught me how to take these steps.

Introduction

8 STEPS TO FINANCIAL FREEDOM

Where does the idea of financial freedom even come from? It is kind of hard to get to the origin of this concept. But I will tell you here what it means to me. As far as I am concerned, being financially free is being able to live your one precious life in the way you choose, without having to rely on work per se or on "a job" to provide you with the income you want. Nor does it mean having to wait until a certain age to have enough money to live in a way that is truly aligned to your purpose and passions. You really can have the resources and flexibility that you desire—even in these crazy times.

Traditionally, the idea of financial freedom begins with retirement. The very concept of retirement dates to the 1920s when it was used to attract workers to America's industrial sector with promises of later-life support. In 1935, the Social Security Act was passed with the official retirement age set at 65, although the average worker age was significantly below that at the time. Fast forward to today, and there are now more than 54 million retirees in the USA. But are they financially free?

It doesn't seem so, with many working well into their retirement years to pay for their basic needs.

Perhaps this notion of being financially free is today circling around the idea of FIRE: Financial Independence, Retire Early. This is a modern movement, and the goal is to save and invest between 50 and 75% of your income by aggressively putting money away so you can retire in your 30s or 40s. Shredding life's abundance or material items to live simply and without much expense are part of this philosophy of being free. But without the resources to connect to the desires or dreams you may have, is that really being free? And does saving aggressively really get you to where you want to go?

A DIFFERENT VISION

I wanted to write a book about achieving financial freedom in a different way, something that wasn't wedded to the vision of necessarily retiring later in life, living on a golf course, and relaxing in the sun if you are one of the lucky ones. This idea is focused more on creating an opportunity for yourself and your family that affords you to truly be free: to have the time and resources to invest in the things that you hold closely to your heart. Perhaps you have been keeping quiet with your dreams lately because life hasn't quite turned out as you expected. Maybe your career has left you a bit unfulfilled or hasn't translated into the financial, intellectual, or emotional capital that you were hoping for.

I want to examine the idea that regardless of your stage of life, you can create net wealth outside of retirement accounts or Social Security income—today. There really is no need to wait for the "right time." You can create this wealth with assets that generate passive income, so you no longer need to be reliant on an employer or business. You can effectively leave the grind of the 9-to-5 behind you, and still create the kind of lifestyle you desire.

Right now, you really can invest in the resources and skills you acquired in your 30s, 40s, or 50s to define the next chapter in your life that you can carry forward into your retirement years, without having to wait until you are 65. **Financial freedom is the idea that you are free to fulfil your goals and wishes for yourself and to really turn your dreams into reality.**

I want to stress right from the start that I am not a financial advisor, and my background may or may not be that different from yours. I grew up in a small town in the Midwest, with a population of around 6,000 people. The typical career path there is to go into manufacturing or to become a farmer. My father was a teacher of history and American political systems. He certainly didn't have the answer for everything, but he stressed the importance of hard work, discipline, education, and an appreciation of history to figure out what might be going on in the world and what to do next. Not surprisingly, I bought into the ideals of studying hard, getting a good education, and taking some risks early on, to then settle predictably into the societal norm of a "career."

However, about 10 years into this respectable career, I was faced with a rather uncomfortable reality. Quite simply, I needed something more to life than just the latest title, promotion, or simple financial reward for giving up my time for an employer's agenda and set of values. I craved a different path, but I just wasn't sure what it was; but I didn't want to spend the rest of my life working for someone else. This might have been a bit of my maternal grandfather's blood coming through, as he had jumped ship to start his own business in his 40s. But instead of setting up my own company, I wanted to learn more about investing and creating net wealth to replace my earned income. I just loved the idea that I could create an enviable lifestyle for myself, and have time to invest in my true passions, whatever they turned out to be.

To be honest, I wasn't sure where to start. I mean, it's not as if this idea of financial freedom was ever taught in school, nor did I personally know anyone who had achieved this goal. Of course, I had read books by people who had managed this feat, but I really hadn't come across anyone else who was planning to embark on a road to financial freedom in quite the same way (that is, by building net wealth to replace earned income).

As I soon discovered, the expensive cars, homes, and trips round the world are really the preserve of celebrities and people who have inherited great wealth, and they didn't come readily to people on the path that I had chosen. I would later discover that the journey I had opted for would require humility, sacrifice, and new principles to live by that completely went against the consumption culture that surrounds us.

So, I wanted to pull back the curtain a bit and share my own experience as someone who started out with a respectable job and a clearly defined career path. But like many people, whether they admit to it or not, I was perhaps a bit unfulfilled, and I wanted to try something different, and to have the resources to grow into the person I wanted to become. I decided to go after financial freedom while well into my career. I was in my mid 30s when I started. Looking back, I wish I had begun a lot earlier, but I think the timing was right. I had the right balance in my life to create and execute my mission. As I approached the final stages of this plan, I wanted to share with you the steps I have taken to get there along with some suggestions and helpful to-dos to guide you through the process.

As I have already mentioned, I am not a certified financial advisor, nor do I come from a family of investors; I'm just a regular working professional who had dreams of doing bigger things with my life. I wanted to write a book on this subject from the perspective of someone other than a financial professional who has walked the walk. There are too many books written by experts and analysts that seem to espouse financial theories or philosophies but are short on practical, personal experiences. I just wonder how many "free" people there are out there, working in the financial world, who are not living by their own advice. I am sure some do but judging by the numbers of people now living from paycheck to paycheck, and losing all sight of their dreams, real-life mentors are thin on the ground. And so, as a first-generation financially free pioneer who made a ton of mistakes and learned plenty of lessons along the way, I wanted to share these steps with you.

Part One

GETTING YOUR HOUSE IN ORDER

1

FIRST STEP: DEFINING WHAT IT'S ALL FOR

What's it all for anyway? What's your "*Why*, "your purpose? I used to get very confused by this question when I was younger. As a kid, my *why* was to eat, sleep, get my schoolwork done as soon as possible, and then go and hang out with my friends. As I got a little bit older, I was then caught up into societal *Whys* such as getting a good education, landing a decent job, working hard, saving, settling down, and having a family; ticking off these things seemed to guarantee you a life of purpose and happiness.

Or did it? If like me you have experienced the loss of a loved one at a relatively young age, it shakes up your belief systems and causes you to look at the world in a completely different way. I was only in my 20s, when I really started to question my purpose and to ask myself over again: what's all this for?

WHAT'S YOUR PURPOSE?

I remember arriving at a point in life where I had accomplished a considerable amount having earned two graduate degrees, building a good career in biopharmaceuticals, owning a house on the golf course and two cars, working a great job, and having no debt. Although at that stage I wasn't really doing anything to increase my wealth or to create my future financial independence. I was living an affluent lifestyle. I also had plenty of solid friends, and I had overcome the death of my beloved father, whom I lost when I was only 25. And yet, I still felt troubled as to what life was about. Without getting too spiritual or religious, it was only when one of my closest friends invited me into his church, the Denver Community Church, that I started reconnecting again with my sense of purpose.

I think it was the combination of biblical readings, self-help books, and having time to reflect that really led me to focus on my mission in life. I had no idea if other people were also having these conversations with themselves, but at the time, everyone else looked as if they were quite happily getting on with their lives. At least, that's how it seemed.

But as I spent more and more time dwelling on my purpose, a clear vision of my mission in life began to emerge. There were recurrent themes of service, helping others, coaching, mentoring, and assisting people to achieve their dreams and ambitions. All these things, I began to realize, were very much connected to my purpose. The times when I felt the most stimulated in life were always around growth of some sort, whether it was spiritual, mental, or physical. I loved learning new things, travelling, exploring new cultures, and discovering buried skills and talents. All these things brought me the greatest satisfaction. I realized then that perhaps my *why* was to serve others through my ability to grow skills and knowledge.

With every year that passed, my sense of purpose became clearer, and I now know that my *why* is to serve those less fortunate than myself, especially youngsters who have been dealt a tough hand. And that is why I have mentored kids through Big Brothers Big Sisters of America, coached with the Special Olympics, and served at rescue missions. I am always looking for organizations to get involved with that will help others to get through hardships and challenges and really make something of their lives.

It is strange, though, how society can push back on your life's purpose. Perhaps this is something you have also encountered. When you start questioning the direction you want to take, other people might respond with stock phrases like, "You do enough," or "You should be happy with what you have," or "Keep doing what you're doing." It seems strange to me that people can't appreciate that not all of us want to live our lives in the same way. Perhaps some people simply don't have the time or energy to create a different plan, and that's fine. But this shouldn't put you off. I knew I needed to pursue a framework to create financial freedom if I really wanted to be happy, and I also knew I'd need help getting there, and so I started looking more closely at the people I was spending my time with.

DISCOVER YOUR *WHY*

Getting closer to my *Why*, at least financially, hit when I was listening to a podcast on real estate investing and reading a few books on retiring early. I was sort of kicking around this idea of financial freedom in my mid-30s. I had always been very invested in learning more about personal finance, and by then, I had covered the basics of a debt-free life and was looking for more information, so I wanted to see what I could find. Each author, I discovered, emphasised how important it was to have a clear *Why* when undertaking a financial journey. It was

THE thing that was emphasized the most, although to be honest, I wasn't sure what they were referring to at the time.

Later, as I ploughed deeper into my financial journey plan, it dawned on me. The direction I was taking wasn't going to be easy or straightforward. It required a lot of sacrifice and extra work, and it meant going against the grain and living in a very different way from most other people. To sustain myself and to keep on track, I needed to be clear on my reasons for what I was doing—my *Why* had to be at the very forefront of my mind.

I needed to really know why I was bucking the trend and investing in such a different vision for my future. Heck, it would be just so easy to follow the crowd, and once I'd done my time, just join all the other retirees somewhere sunny. Or sadly, what's becoming more of a reality is to just keep working. Neither of these options appealed to me; I just wanted something different. I wanted the time and space while I was still young enough to make the most of it, to become the kind of person I wanted to be. I knew I didn't want to work for 40 years for someone else. Instead, I wanted more time to focus on the things I love like my family, adventure, travel, other jobs, or careers that were more interesting than my current one. And I didn't necessarily want to give up everything around me to try to engage in those renewed interests later in life.

Once I had established my *why* I realized it was important for me to write it down. That way, I would have the focus to start breaking down the steps that would lead me to financial freedom. This would allow me to come up with strategies and tactics to move along the journey; it would give me a framework to celebrate the victories and to learn and grow from the challenges. It would hold me in check when I became overwhelmed or impatient with the big dream of independence. It would also act as a GPS system as I made crucial decisions on my way: choices related to my cost of living, income and expenses, and investment strategies. These, I believed, would all become much clearer to me, if they were connected to my purpose. Your *Why* can be that fuel you need to move to the next step. And the steps in this book can help guide you towards the finish line.

REALLY REFLECT ON LIFE

When I was younger, this idea about purpose seemed to be defined or influenced greatly by my parents. My grandfather and father had the most influence on me. My mother became sick when I was still very young and would struggle with her health for the rest of her life, and I never knew my biological father. My stepdad, or just "Dad" to me, really had the right instincts as a parent. He taught me discipline, hard work, commitment to try new things, and perseverance—all essential tools for achieving some success in life, whatever that might mean. My maternal grandfather was a successful businessman, and he owned a small regional logistical company in the south. He was also a decorated WW2 hero.

I looked up to my grandfather, who had grown up poor in rural Texas and had lived through the Depression and so many other challenges of the twentieth century. Nevertheless, he had used his natural charm and instincts to build up his small business after the war, and he taught me how to deal with people so I could get the best out of them. He had this totally genuine way of making others feel important, so they naturally gravitated towards him. Anyway, I digress. Although I was greatly influenced by my grandfather, as a teenager, I wouldn't say I had my own *Why.* Well, other than the usual: hoping to be liked and loved by the people around me and wanting to be a good son and make my family proud.

It wasn't until I was in my mid-20s that my *Why* really surfaced. At the time, I was an actor living in Southern California, and I was in the mist of graduating with a degree in performance art when I received the call that my father, my best friend, had cancer. He was only 54. He had only a few months to live, and I rushed to be by his side to spend precious time with him. On my flight, I recall pulling out a pad of paper and pen and writing down the questions I wanted to ask. It was difficult. I had never lost someone I loved before, and every time I tried to think about what I wanted to ask him, my mind would go blank. A couple of questions I did ask were: How can I be a better son in the future? What did you cherish the most in your life? My father and I talked through my questions, and he challenged me to think bigger. He inspired me to keep exploring, knowing that I was strong enough and smart enough to find my purpose. His own, he confessed, had been me and my brother and sister, and his 35 years of teaching and coaching. This had been his *Why.* And it made sense because he had taught and coached not only his own children, but thousands of kids over the years.

After reflecting on these conversations and once the grieving process had taken hold, I had started to discover a new kind of *Why.* I soon got an additional degree and took on a real career with a real job. That would certainly have made my father proud.

Fast forward to my mid-30s, and there I was in a 3,500-square-foot house on a golf course, with a couple of cars, no debt, good friends, and close family, yet I was struggling with my *Why* again. It was weird; I had checked all the right boxes and yet I still felt unfulfilled. Don't get me wrong—I was thankful for the success I'd had. But I couldn't shy away from that empty feeling, and it wasn't until one of my closest friends encouraged me to head back to church that I began to gain some clarity. I had grown up Catholic, but I hadn't felt tempted to reconnect with my childhood faith, believing that religion wasn't my spiritual purpose. But suddenly, this new church I had joined felt right. Perhaps it was the heartfelt readings, or the uplifting pastor, or the supportive community, but it deeply stirred something in me.

Soon after I joined the church, I found myself mentoring some disadvantaged kids, and I coached them in different sports. The ideas of service and growth were starting to resonate strongly with me, and as I began spending more time with my family and close friends, it occurred to me that helping those around me was much more fun than working all the time. I was travelling a lot too, another great passion of mine (I have now been to 84 different countries, and my aim is to get to every sovereign state on the planet). I began to imagine what life would be like if I had more time than my two weeks of annual leave. Discovering new cultures has always left me with a renewed wonder for the world, as I find visiting new places gives me perspective and an appreciation of how different people live, and I couldn't help wondering what it would be like being able to invest in those experiences more often. My *Why* finally seemed to be taking on a new form, only this time, it was purely defined by me.

I wish I could say that I have finally nailed it, that I have all the answers to my *Why*. But as I sit here today in my mid-40s, I can tell you that my *Why* continues to evolve. But it's mine now, and I'm passionate about getting even deeper with it. My process of tapping into my *Why* is now broken down into the various elements of my own life. From a spiritual perspective, I connect with my creator, with God and pray intently to learn how I can best serve. My health and physical state are critical given my sense of service, growth, and adventure, and knowing my *Why* requires me to have a strong body and mobility long into my life. My career has carried me so far, but the deeper I get into my *Why*, the more time I'll need away from a concept of just a career, from simply having someone else determine my days. My financial freedom is a must, not to get rich, but to be wealthy in terms of time and resources, so that I can help those less fortunate, and be able to do the things that need to get done to make the type of difference I would like to make.

The combination of my enriching upbringing, my experience traveling the world, and working in various industries has blessed me with the tools to help others in different ways. The more I can grow with new activities, hobbies, and experiences, the more I can relate to others and help them to achieve their dreams, too. That is my *Why*, and it's something that I can own, something that puts energy into my day and is big enough for me to press through the challenges towards achieving financial independence.

No one else will get me towards my goal or you towards yours. It is not like a work project or getting the groceries—tasks with specific deadlines that need to be accomplished. Your sense of *Why* will need to keep pushing you forward. Ultimately, though, it's up to you whether you achieve financial freedom and get the chance to become the person you truly want to be.

DIG DEEP

At this point, you might be tempted to skip the rest of the chapter. Perhaps you just want to get to the steps towards financial freedom and to skip all this fluffy *Why* stuff. Right? But this questioning and analysis really is an essential part of the process, so don't take any shortcuts. I see far too many people who have all the resources, but simply don't have the time or self-knowledge to make a difference. Their *Why* just isn't evolved enough for them to be able to take that first step. Their lives might well be steady and comfortable, but they're still unhappy. This is something you might have experienced too—I know I certainly did.

But by taking time to understand what motivates you, the next steps will be much clearer. First though, let me ask you this question once again. You've already made sacrifices and had your struggles to arrive at where you are today. So, do you *really* know why you are doing this? The way our education system is structured suggests that we should have our purpose figured out by the time we reach our 20s. But what if things change as we get older? Are we supposed to just suck it up, get through life, and blindly hope for retirement one day? Or is there another way? I am telling you that there most definitely is—and it starts with you.

At this early stage, it is all about determining your *Why.* And there are lots of different authors out there and techniques to help you dig deeper into your own personal motivations. I am not here to endorse one method over another as what worked for me might not work for you. The important thing is to pick a strategy and to get started without too much delay. Some of my close family and friends got very caught up in the thinking stage of their *Why* yet still struggled to define what was motivating them. But I now know from experience that you don't get any answers just from thinking. What worked for me was nature walks, meditation, and reading some inspirational books. Simon Sinek is a great author who covers this subject extensively in his book *Start with Why.*

To help achieve clarity, it is worth asking yourself some questions once you are "in the zone." Really try and think what in life excites and inspires you. For me, my heart gets pumping when I'm thinking of the things that I would to do if I had plenty of time and was in complete control of my schedule. I constantly ask myself what my life would be like if I had the chance to spend my days in activities that were 100% aligned to my values. For example, my father taught American Political Systems in high school, and I even had him as a teacher, so whenever I'm involved in our political process here in the USA, such as helping at the polls during election, I feel that passion and physical sensation of being aligned to my values. Helping to ensure that everyone has a chance to voice their support for their leaders really makes me feel alive. It's the same when I hear from people I have mentored in the past, and they tell me how well they are doing now. Or a former mentee recalls some of my advice that helped. That really does bring tears to my eyes because it means I have been able to make a difference.

But are we only supposed to have a few of those life-affirming days? What if we could have them more often? What if you and I both had more time and resources to invest in those things? Now take the time to ask yourself, if time or money were not an issue for you, how would you spend your days? This is an exercise I do monthly, so I am constantly appraising and updating my *Why*. Whatever methods you use to delve deeper into your purpose make sure you use them often. It sounds simple, but so few people seem to take the time to do this. And yet, it will likely be the thing that propels you through the ups and downs in your wealth-building years to come.

WRITE IT DOWN

Once you have come up with a clear vision of your *Why* make sure you write it down. Some people use vision boards, others have journals, some have notes jotted into their phone to reference. Whichever works for you, just make sure it's something you frequently revisit, almost on a weekly basis. After all, you don't just want to have that aching *Why* in your heart, you want to be able to apply it to the various areas of your life as well.

This might sound silly, but I have had this Excel document for roughly 10 years, and in it, I have broken up my life into different sections (spiritual, health, family/friends, career, finances, adventure, and activities). Each section has a set of short-, medium-, and long-term goals associated with it. I revisit this document on a weekly basis to keep things updated and to inspire me to update my personal journals so that I can continue to write things down and to monitor my progress. These goals aren't just financial either. I work hard to make sure they all line up to my personal *Why* too. I have specific goals written down for my own personal health, so that I am in strong physical shape to travel, to meet new people, and to take on the tasks that are required to serve and help others. My spreadsheet also includes specific goals that I need to achieve for my career that test and align to my overall purpose; that way, my personal *Why* can also be applied to my job.

There are goals I want to achieve in adventure and activities, so that I have a better idea of where to invest my time when more of it becomes available when I am financially free. Think through the different aspects of your life; don't wait until you achieve freedom in your future to make these decisions. Once you are free, you want to be able to put your *Why* into action as quickly as you can.

Now that you've captured where you are with your own personal *Why* and have it well documented to refer to and to hold yourself accountable, be sure to share it with close family and friends, those who believe in you and your mission and have your best personal interests in mind. I would suggest you be selective, however, and only share this information with those people who truly have your back and want you to achieve your ultimate happiness. Family isn't always the best source of support with a project like this. They might not understand the importance of you discovering *Why* or of achieving financial freedom. That's okay; some of them might come around once you are further down the road. The thing is it will probably be your family's instinct to protect you, and they might be concerned that you are opting to take the road less travelled. This might look to you at first like a lack of support, but really, it is most probably just a concern.

Of course, there might be people who feel threatened by what you are trying to do, and they may well be operating from a position of jealousy or fear. And that's okay. Just be picky who you share your plans with. You only really want to involve people who appreciate your sense of purpose and respect your *Why* too. I have a close friend whom I have known for a long time. He's unique; after each conversation we have, I feel even more on fire. He not only encourages me to get after my *Why* but also provides me with further insights and examples of what he is doing in his own life, and this encourages me to go even further. I am so blessed to have him in my life. Cherish these supportive friendships and invest in those relationships that really bring extra meaning to your life.

The steps you need to take to capture your own purpose might seem straightforward, but that doesn't make them any less important. Remember to write things down and to share your goals with the right people. This might all sound simple in principle, but it's the execution that is key. It takes time to capture this sense of purpose in your heart and to ensure that it is very clearly defined in your head before moving forward.

Financial freedom might well be something that many people desire, but when they discover how hard it is to achieve, they then fall back into societal norms. But financial freedom doesn't have to be something that only a few people can achieve; it can be something for you and me to aspire to as well. I'm not going to say it will be easy, especially if you are a "first generation" pioneer or the first person in your family to embark on this journey. But your *Why* will most definitely keep you on track and will sustain you through all the ups and downs along the way. Take the time to capture it, keep it alive, and keep it with you—and now, let's get started.

2

SECOND STEP: GETTING READY

I'm not sure if you've had a similar experience, but once I started to see some success in building my wealth, or reaching some interim goals towards my financial freedom, I began to receive phone calls from close family, friends, and even some acquaintances. They wanted my advice, and I was and still am genuinely happy to help; in fact, I always feel inspired when other people decide to go for it. Perhaps this is something you are witnessing too. Other people have noticed how your financial thinking has evolved, and they want to pick your brain about what they should do to get closer to their own personal freedom goals.

Now, I'm always humbled by these requests if they come my way. After all, I'm still executing my plan and have a bit to go. But it's good to connect and to discuss these ideas with other people. When I have these conversations, I consistently go through the list of steps outlined in this book to try and figure out how I can best guide them, or I refer them to a professional in that specific area of the journey. Often the conversation will start with them telling me they have some spare money to invest, and they want to know how I would proceed. My initial response to this question is to ask, "What is it that you are trying to achieve?"

And that really is when the conversation can become a little stuck, and the person in front of me or on the other end of the phone seems to become a bit baffled. I'm not sure why this is; perhaps it's because they haven't been asked this question in a while, or they are trying to connect the advice they are seeking to the question I have asked. I'll typically get an answer around saving for something specific or to add to their retirement fund. As I dig a bit deeper, they may say things like, "Greater security for my family," "Protection if I lose my job," or even, "I want to start my own business or non-profit." And that's a great first step, as I then know where they are heading.

BE READY

From there, I try to determine if their house is in order. What I mean by this is simply whether their personal balance sheet is, in fact, balanced. I ask them if they are spending less than they are earning and if they have paid off any bad debts and have enough put away in emergency savings. The truth is before anyone can really think about investing or working towards financial freedom, they need to plug any holes in the ship, because otherwise, the entire plan will sink.

It is at this point that I can sense the other person is getting frustrated. They just want to cut to the chase, and get a few investment tips, but I tell them they need to put in the work to get their house in order first before I can help. Okay, this might sound harsh, but I would be acting irresponsibly if I helped them to speed ahead as doing so would completely derail their entire plan. For instance, what happens if someone starts investing, and then the car needs replacing, or their boiler breaks down? If they don't have the money put aside, they will need to disrupt their wealth plan to cover the costs, and the whole thing will be thrown into disarray.

Before I offer any investment advice, I really encourage people to identify any holes in the balance sheet, and then to check that they have honestly adopted certain behaviors that will ensure they are ready to move onto the next step. Below we will examine some of the healthy financial habits that need to be in place before you can start building wealth and a couple of the negative behaviors that might get in the way.

STOP COMPARING

Spending less than you earn sounds like such a simple concept, and yet, it is surprising how many people over-extend themselves. They are caught up in a comparative world with their colleagues, friends, and neighbors, who are themselves not living below their means. I'm not sure where all this showmanship stems from, but in the Western world, it certainly seems to seep into our consciousness at an early age. When I was younger, I would often compare my successes and failures with those of my siblings, which is silly, really, as we are all on our own unique journey and have such different skills and abilities.

It seems as if success or the likelihood of someone "making it" is benchmarked by going to a highly ranked college and landing a good job with a nice title and benefits package and having an enviable lifestyle.

REDUCE SPENDING

And yet, many people who have achieved these things on the outside are struggling on the inside, both financially and emotionally. Some families break up under the strain of financial pressure; other people might seem to have ticked all the right boxes, but on the inside, they feel unfulfilled and empty, sort of like I did. They might try to fill this void by buying more things, seeking greater promotions and titles, and so it goes.

Part of the process of putting your house in order will be taking the time to really reset what you value and how you want to spend your time. And if financial freedom is the ticket to your *Why,* you'll need to get used to living below your means, whatever stage you are at in life. It may not have to be according to the FIRE rules (financially independent, retire early), which is based on aggressive savings goals and getting rid of a lot of things; but it will require stepping back from the pressures of today's society and turning away from the consumption culture. If you honestly want to become financially free, it is your behavior you must change.

At the end of the day, it's all about having more income left over by month's end than what is being taken away in expenses. And those big-ticket items such as housing, transportation, taxes, food, and debt will need to be adjusted.

DELAYED GRATIFICATION

Delayed gratification is the idea that you give up something today for a more prosperous future. Now, this sacrifice to essentially delay gratification to achieve a better tomorrow will undoubtedly challenge you. Your friends and colleagues will spend their hard-earned money differently than you. They will splash out on the latest car, take a gamble on a hot stock, live in an expensive area of town, and take many vacations complete with postings on social media. You may well feel under pressure from family and friends to give in and to live for the day. As I write, we are in the middle of a pandemic. Isn't that a good reason to buy yourself some added comfort? My answer is yes, but only if you can afford to do so without compromising your long-term plan. My beloved father died when he was only 54, and he never got the chance to retire, and I have lost friends before their time too. So, I know the importance of enjoying life, and this year I am organising a big family trip to the Rockies. So, I'm not saying you completely put your life on hold. Instead, just spend wisely.

Mentally, you must stay strong when various news feeds and marketing campaigns entice you to spend more. You will need to control those urges, those comparisons, those weak moments when you're tired of living in a crummy house or driving a 15-year-old vehicle. It is hard to live so frugally when you are making good money and have a successful career. It's only human nature to want to show off about how well you are doing, but this is an instinct that you will need to resist. I honestly do get this. Currently, I am driving an 11-year-old car with 105,000 miles on the odometer. I live in a small town home in a retirement community near my workplace. Recently, one of my colleagues jokingly asked me if the firm was paying me enough. I laughed as I knew where he was coming from; before my financial freedom journey, I too was concerned about what people thought of my car, house, or clothes, but now I couldn't care less. What my co-worker doesn't know is that I am plowing my savings into assets that will soon give me the choice whether to work or not. In all honesty, it does still suck sometimes! But I keep focusing on my *Why* and knowing that I will have so many choices in the future; which makes the sacrifices I am making now easier to cope with.

LIVING BELOW YOUR MEANS

An integral part of delayed gratification is the ability to live significantly below your means. I currently live 80% below my income, which when I write it down does sound drastic, but it works for me. You need to bear in mind that my circumstances might be quite different from yours. I have a well-paid, full-time job, and I live alone. I don't have children of my own, although my girlfriend has two teenage daughters, and I do try to help with their needs as they arise. Really, you need to be honest about what you are trying to achieve, and how much you can realistically put aside. One positive consequence of the pandemic is that people seem to be saving more: the average savings rate in the USA in 2021 is hovering around 13%, while in Europe, it's 16%. But I would suggest you need to be saving at least 40% of your income to really build up wealth. Another consequence of the pandemic is the growing acceptance of remote work, which should save us all time and money in the long run.

Saving effectively does take quite a bit of planning. I use an offline version of Excel to track my yearly and monthly spending but there are other helpful applications out there, such as Mint. Perhaps you can start with a list of all your income and outgoings and then take an inventory of the last 6 to 8 months and lay it out against your net income. I must stress here that it is important only to look at your *net total*, not your gross income. The gross figure will not help you to get to living below your needs, which you will need to move forward. So, as you are looking at your monthly net income from your job and other earnings minus your monthly living expenses (such as your mortgage or rent, car expenses, insurance, credit cards, groceries, entertainment, travel, utilities, subscriptions, and any other costs) did you break even?

This exercise is like taking a very cold shower in the morning. It will really wake you up! The truth is if you don't save, you will never have the life you want, or to quote financial guru Alvin Hall, "Unless you are capable of saving, you'll have little chance to ever enjoy real prosperity, let alone wealth."

When I first started thinking about financial freedom, I was living barely under my net income for the month, and I was only saving 10% of my income despite being on a good salary. Perhaps it is your housing costs, your bad debt, or those car payments that are making it so difficult for you to put anything aside. If you live in the USA, you can give your finances a boost by moving out of a city that charges a city wage tax. No matter where you are from, moving to a cheaper area is always an option if you want to save more. These are tough choices, there's no doubt about it. And for some of you it might just be a case of cancelling a few subscriptions. Others may need to take much more drastic measures such as getting rid of their car or not going on holiday.

By moving across the country into a lower state tax area, I significantly increased my net income and drastically lowered my monthly expenses; along with it came reduced daily spending, and I cut out many of my monthly subscriptions. Yet I continued to hold onto the things that I enjoy doing such as going to the gym and keeping some streaming services.

There really are some unexpected benefits to all these sacrifices. By making a more conscious choice of where I lived, I lowered my car insurance payments and reduced my utility bills too. And because I moved into a rapidly developing area, full of newly retired folks, my equity has gone up substantially on the house. Your sacrifice or moves may not need to be as drastic as mine were, but you will have to make some tough decisions. The funny thing is, after a while, those things you held onto will start to feel less important.

FIND YOUR TRIBE

Another change you need to make to get your house in order is to try and spend as much time as you can with people whose financial goals are closely aligned to your own. I am not saying you can't spend time with people who are big spenders. In fact, I have a lot of young friends who really embrace the You Only Live Once (YOLO) philosophy, and don't really understand why I am choosing to live such a Spartan life in my 40s. I admire their spontaneity and live-for-the-day mentality, but I know how much I crave financial freedom, so I'm not deterred.

But for those really close to you, it is important that they respect your goals. They don't have to agree with all the details but having someone in your corner is a huge advantage and is so much better than being on different sides of "the game of life." If your partner is very much a "live free" person, and you're trying to build wealth, it might be much harder to achieve your plan.

You would be surprised at the number of real estate investors, financial advisors, attorneys, property managers, and so-called experts who are just living their lives like everyone else and have very little to speak of in net wealth. It wasn't until my mid-30s that I sought to mainly surround myself with family and friends who didn't just value "things" in life but wanted "experiences." I loved the wonderful conversations I would have with them, the talk of serving others, and how we would spend our time and resources to help people, all the things that aligned with my *Why*. Yes, it's okay to live the good life and to focus on all the things you would like, but if that's all the conversation is about—latest promotion, bonus, extension to the house, latest model of a car—then none of this is going to result in financial independence.

I would suggest taking some time, maybe a few hikes outside in your favorite park, and doing a mental inventory of all the people in your life. Perhaps ask yourself who remembers your birthday, and who, at work, would reach out to you if you were no longer working there. Who in your life has been there for you over the years, regardless of your success?

Who in your family loves you and wants what you want, not what *they* want? And who do you need to cut out (or at least take in small doses)? Once you have this sorted, it's important to start surrounding yourself with those people who will be with you on this journey.

And you'll need to put the work into reaching out, calling, scheduling Zoom meetings, and spending quality time with them. Take an active interest in their lives. They'll let you know what you're up to, but you'll need quality people and quality time with them in your life. Get your support team ready, primed, and ready to roll!

CHANGE YOUR LIFESTYLE

So, those are just a few behaviors to ensure your house is in order; there are more, I am sure. But if you can get used to living well below your means, you'll have the foundation to support you on your journey. To do this you are probably going to have to make some significant lifestyle changes, and this won't be easy. Believe me, I know. I made the tough decision to move from an incredible location in Southern California, where I was making good money at my regular job, to a different part of the country where I knew few people. But that move gave me a greater opportunity to chase my financial independence.

It wasn't easy, I remember waking up thinking, "What did I do?" Those sunsets in California…well, I'll always miss those. But to accelerate my net wealth building plan, to have my own financial freedom within reach, to have all the time and adequate resources to fulfil my personal *Why*, well, that was worth it, that's worth *anything*, as those things are invaluable.

When I arrived at that point where my *Why* was the clearest it had ever been—to be free financially and to use my skills and knowledge on other initiatives that had more to do with my personal passion—I wanted to run towards my goal, head straight to Go, and collect my $200 (an image for you Monopoly fans out there). But I soon realized I would need to make some more changes in my life to get there, although my behaviors were not that bad. I had always worked hard, starting at an early age as a bus boy at the local pancake house and in high school as a waiter at the local Pizza Hut. Considering the tips, those were good jobs. I opened a checking and savings account early on and was a good steward of my money. After college and even graduate school, I paid off my student loans, purchased a home, and had a company car and my own personal vehicle, all without incurring any debt. But outside of my retirement account, I was a long way from financial freedom, and I knew I had to accelerate my investments if I wanted to get there sooner rather than later.

My goal was to accelerate my wealth-building significantly over a span of 5 to 6 years, which would equate to some of my peak earning years at the lowest cost of living rates in my entire life. And it would take just a few bold changes.

I had worked my way up the ladder, so to speak, of the biopharmaceuticals industry that I joined 17 years before (after first working as an actor and then spending a year in academia). Throughout my current career, I have had 15 different positions, and I have lived in 10 different locations across the USA and Europe. All this movement might not appeal to some people, but it was always my aim to learn as much as I could and to add as much value as possible to my employer. My goal was to become a well-rounded and innovative employee, and to get there has involved sacrifice, as I have worked hard to build up successful teams in large corporations and small companies alike.

As I have already mentioned, when I really discovered my *Why*, I was living in one of the most beautiful places in the USA, perhaps in the world, a place surrounded by cliffside beaches, stunning sunsets, and expensive things. Life was good, but it came at quite a cost. Just renting in Southern California can easily cost $3,000 per month, and that's just for a one-bedroom apartment. High taxes (they call them the "sunshine tax") all added to that high cost of living. And as tempting as it was to stay, I knew I would never get to my *Why* living there, so I moved to a much cheaper part of the country where I hardly knew anyone. Although I enjoyed my new job, in other areas of my life, I really had to start over.

And financially, it worked! I significantly reduced my cost of living all while maintaining and even increasing my income. I bought a simple town home in a booming area and started living 80% below my means. My reduced cost of living allowed me to accelerate the investments that I had begun to build. At that point, I thought I was well on my way, but there were still a few more things I needed to change.

BUILD RESILIENCE

Mentally, I was tough. I had been through a lot growing up and have overcome many challenges. I was a man of great faith and purpose. I was also physically in good shape and developed a healthy habit of working out on a regular basis and making sure I made my regular healthcare appointments. However, I noticed an extra layer of stress building as I grew my net wealth plan. It could have been the worry of taking on new investments and ensuring they made good returns. I needed to ensure my mind was as strong as my spirit and body. When making new investments, there are a lot of unknowns. And there is additional risk when it's your hard-earned money on the line. It can make getting a good night's sleep quite a challenge.

To keep myself calm, I developed regular relaxation techniques such as meditation and journaling. I would also schedule regular meetings with my family and friends, whether they were close by or far away; it was a consistent outreach so that I could share my successes and failures. Just to be told, "You've got this," was enough to keep me going. I also found that the regular practice of writing down what I was grateful for daily really gave me perspective. These would often be simple things, and I also took time to reflect on the priorities I needed to juggle to reach my *Why*.

Most days were small steps along the way, and I celebrated each little victory. Sometimes it felt like everything was moving far too slowly, and I had to learn to be patient and to never lose sight of my *Why*. It hasn't always been easy to make all the sacrifices required, especially in times of political and social turbulence. But each year, I have moved a little closer to financial freedom by remaining focused on the end-game, keeping my house in order, and not being tempted to spend unnecessarily.

KEEP TRACK

This section might be a tough one. It involves some sacrifice, and it is frustrating not being able to jump straight into the numbers that will produce your financial freedom. But it is so essential to get your house in order first. I have seen so many people either get tripped up early on or fall back once things get challenging down the road. So, let's make sure that you're built for the long haul. It's worth putting in the effort now to ensure you get the freedom you crave later.

Let's also make sure you are mentally strong; this is something I'm still working on myself. When the pandemic hit, I noticed an increase in my own anxiety and stress, even though I felt fine at the time. It was important for me to monitor my mental and emotional strength. One of the best ways I have found to do this is journaling, as it enables me to connect my thoughts with my emotions. For example, there is a series of Panda Journals that allows you to record your daily, weekly, and monthly goals and to break down what you are grateful for, what you are excited about, and your priorities for the day, which is very useful. As well as using my Excel spreadsheet to keep track of my spending and saving, it is also useful for charting the journey towards my *Why.* I even use color codes to hold myself accountable on all areas of my progress.

This is a trick my dad taught me at a very early age. I was a swimmer, and we had a leader board in our laundry room with all the individual events listed and our personal best times. When we improved that time, we would update it with a Sharpie and stencils. It might sound weird, but it works! I also use yoga and meditation to boost my mental strength, and neither of them came easily to me as I'm not very flexible, and my mind is always ready to wander. But I persevered, and I now practise yoga and meditate every day, and I am far more relaxed and better at controlling my thoughts. The sense of balance and health that both these things have given me are priceless. Most certainly, with the added stress of the journey you are about to take, you'll need to focus on your mental health, and know how to let the non-essential things go, and to drown out all the noise from the people who matter least to you.

So now you've got a solid *Why* well documented and close to you, you've taken the steps to get your house in order with some sacrifices to button up your day-to-day living expenses, and you have prepared yourself mentally and surrounded yourself with the right people to start this journey towards freedom. You are edging closer to your goal.

3

THIRD STEP: GOTTA SAVE

Oh boy, another chapter on saving. That's just what you wanted, right? But as I have already stressed, it is important that you follow the lessons in the first half of this book before embarking on the wealth-building strategies of the second half. Of course, I don't believe aggressively saving alone will get you towards your goals, nor is it necessarily what you want life to be all about. You will also need to accelerate your growth and take some calculated investment risks to achieve the net wealth you desire to live life on your own terms. But one of the fundamental building blocks is embracing the principle of saving. Sorry, there's no way round it. You just gotta do this.

PUT IT AWAY

Ever since I was a kid, I always had a piggy bank. I enjoyed the moments where I would fill up that jar, take it down to the grocery store, and drop those coins into the slot that would then spit out a piece of paper that I would take to the register and get me some cold hard cash. I had opened a checking and savings account by the age of 14. My father had instilled in me a strong work ethic and encouraged all three of us children to start working at a young age, allowing us to get used to the idea of earning and spending our own money.

Even as a teenager, I never really wanted to spend all my hard-earned money. This might have been due to my upbringing in a small town in the Midwest, where people's values were traditional, or it could just have been because I was stuck inside for half the year because it was always so freezing! But I think the main reason why I was so careful with my earnings came down to how many hours I had spent either mowing lawns, painting houses, busing tables, or waiting on customers over a 20-hour weekend while still in high school. I certainly took pride in seeing the numbers in that bank account rise, and even better, I was seeing the small increase in savings from interest. Back then, I really didn't understand interest rates, but I was fascinated with the idea of growing your money without having to get your hands dirty or put in any extra work.

Although I started saving as a teenager, I didn't really understand how much I should be saving, nor really, what I would do with these savings. At such a young age, I hadn't yet connected with my *Why*. My family didn't have much money and retirement seemed like it was literally a lifetime away, so I had no real way of knowing what to do with my savings; I just had a strong instinct that I should keep building them. Basic concepts of personal finance weren't taught in school and still seem absent from the curriculum today. This is something I feel very strongly needs to change, because not understanding the basics of how money works can have such a detrimental impact on people's lives. If personal finance was taught in a way that could really influence behavioral change it could eliminate decades of personal challenges down the road.

Despite its wealth, the developed world hasn't been good at saving. Before COVID, the savings rate in the United States hovered between 7 and 8% of earnings, which isn't very impressive. But there were several months in 2020 when this shot up to around 30%; it has halved since then to around 13%.[1] Some of these savings have come from the reduction in personal consumption and overall fears about the future. So, will this trend continue? My guess is that things will start to level back to where they were, although there might be a slight lasting change in behavior.

But even if things stay the same, a savings rate of 13% still means that most Americans are saving less than they are paying in tax. According to the latest figures from the Organization for Economic Cooperation and Development's taxing wages report,[2] the average American pays 24% tax on earnings, which is lower than the tax rates of other OECD member nations—so in the USA, we are typically only saving only half of what we are being taxed. This is gloomy reading, but I think it's an important point.

So, what's going on here? Why are we having so many challenges when saving? Is it the economy, is it inflation, is it psychological and cultural programming? It seems that every week I'm reading about how the average person has little in savings to pay for an emergency or little in retirement funds. Recent studies have also revealed that many Americans are giving up on the idea of ever retiring. They simply can't afford to, but why? It's a complex question (for example, many in this age group found their hard-earned assets and home equity wiped out in the economic crash of the early 2000s, and some unscrupulous lenders found themselves in court); however, part of the problem could be attributed to our spending culture, and the fact we can't seem to get our head around the idea of delayed gratification. And that is something you really need to embrace if you want to live on your own terms.

GETTING RID OF DEBT

Dave Ramsey was a guide for me during my debt pay-down years, and today, when I listen to his podcasts, it makes me quite emotional to hear about the dreadful levels of debt that some people get themselves into and the terrible impact that this has on their lives. As a first step, I would suggest that you line your debt up from top to bottom, listing first the debt with the highest interest rate and so on. Then, with your increased savings from budgeting, list the amount of additional income you plan to pay down against the debt with the highest interest rate. Focus first on that highest-interest debt. This will save money on increased interest payments against the highest rate and will allow you to get rid of that bad debt faster. You'll then take down the next bad debt line item with the second highest interest rate, until you have them all covered. It might take 6 months, or it might take a few years to pay everything off, but just keep going.

Now, if you've arrived at the end of this step and have the first three chapters covered, celebrate! But, whatever you do, don't be tempted to jump into the investment part of your strategy quite yet. We haven't finished putting in the groundwork. First, I would strongly encourage you to save enough for 6 months of emergency needs. This is tough, as it will take extra time. But you can do it. As you've brought your bad debt down to zero, I would suggest taking that same income and turning it into a specific emergency savings account, one that you can pivot to snowball those funds you were using to pay down debt into an emergency account. I would even suggest having this in a different savings account than your regular checking and savings. For me, it keeps things separate in my mind.

Bear in mind that most people live paycheck to paycheck, even those who make very good salaries, as they've over stretched with their cost of living and have their investment/debt ratio upside down. It just takes one thing to go wrong—an accident, an unexpected health bill, or the need for a car repair—for most people to reach for that credit card and head further into bad debt. An emergency savings account will create the buffer you need so that you will not need to disrupt the execution of your plan to build net wealth.

A SAVING STRATEGY

So, this is a big one. You cannot pass Go without completing this step. I've seen too many people wanting to jump to that individual investment idea that will finally create that financial wealth they've been dreaming of. Good people, with grand visions to serve society, to spend more time with their family, to increase their learning, or just to get out from under an employer that has placed them in a box. I've seen them want to run before they perfect the crawl by failing to create a successful savings strategy. But you need this in place first, as it will increase the funds that you must snowball to make those all-too-crucial investments. The more you save, the more you invest, and the more you invest, the greater return of compounding and diversification of risk you will create for your future, along with the greater reward you will feel from your savings efforts.

If you really want to achieve financial freedom, **you need to put away almost half of your income**. To do this, you will need to really set aside time to do some math. Time and resources are critical to understanding where you need to maximize and minimize to create the additional income you need during your wealth-building years. It is critical to tally up the inputs and outputs of income and expenses along with the details of where everything is going. So, if my goal is to reach financial independence in 5 to 10 years' time, I need to understand what is keeping my savings rate low. And for me, as an early goal was to at least have my savings rate above what I was outputting in tax;

in other words, I figured I needed to pay myself more than what I'm paying the government.

COMPOUND INTEREST

I've noticed that personal finance, savings, and the idea around compounding are simply not taught anywhere. Very few people experience this type of education unless someone in their family has been successful at it themselves. It's a key principle that will go into our strategies of wealth building later in this book. To illustrate this idea, I'd like to share a comparison between two different savers. One starts to save at a young age of 21, they save $2K a year until they are 27 and then stop. So, essentially, they save $2K per year for 6 years during their 20s, opening an account that earns a 12% return. Meanwhile, the second saver enjoys their 20s and doesn't put anything away. They might live in a nicer apartment, have a new car, or be too busy having a good time to bother themselves with delayed gratification. However, for this person, who chooses to live for the day while they are young, it will take them saving $2K a year for the next 37 years at the same return just to catch the first saver. I know it's some math and hard to get your head around at first, so let's simplify it a little.

The real message I am trying to get across here is that compound interest works according to a snowball effect, as the bank or market pays interest on your deposit, so if you earn 5% annual interest on a deposit of $100, you would the gain $5 in interest after a year. But what would happen the following year? That really is where compounding comes into play. You will earn the same annual interest, but you'll now earn 5% on $105. So how do you get this to work to your advantage? I am going to shout a little here: **start early and keep saving!**

The earlier you start (remember, leave the money untouched), the more it will accelerate or snowball because compound interest grows exponentially over time. Let's try another example, this time with three savers, let's call them James, Jennifer, and Sam, who each saved $1,000 a month at a rate of 7% for 10 years. Wouldn't you expect them to all end up with the same amount by the age of 65? Well, it doesn't work like this, as compound interest builds up over time. This means that James, who invested between the ages of 25 and 35, earned $1.45M, while Jennifer who invested between 35 and 45 earned $735K, and Sam who invested between the ages of 45 and 55, ended up with $373K.

It's like magic, isn't it? Do make sure you share this with your kids, and don't assume they are learning this kind of thing at school. And although you might not be in your 20s anymore, the concept of delayed gratification will pay off in your net wealth building plan regardless of your age and when you start. I didn't start until my 30s, and my finish line is within reach today. You can do this.

DO YOUR RESEARCH

Spend some time looking at different savings accounts. Open a basic college savings plan for your kids. In the USA, this is known as a 529. Get yourself an employer matched retirement plan. They are a great way of taking advantage of compound interest, although you can't touch the money until you reach retirement age. Really get this idea of delayed gratification right into your head: to really save, you'll need to make some changes to your inputs and outputs. Having more savings not only works, but when you invest those savings into wealth building strategies, they will only compound over time. But it's the daily behavioral changes that you personally make that will eventually alter the way in which you think about money that will matter the most. If you start with wealth-building strategies first, without building key principles of delayed gratification, you'll be fighting an uphill battle and may never cross that finish line towards independence.

During my current wealth-building years, I have saved roughly two-thirds of my income over the last 12 years, and it's mainly due to delayed gratification and pulling back on the outputs. (I honestly haven't bought any new clothes in 5 years.) This allows me to pay myself twice as much as I pay in tax. Those things that you gave up in the short term might not be missed as much later. You might never want those things again as you set your sights firmly on financial freedom.

PEER PRESSURE

In the USA, and indeed, in much of the industrialized world, we really buy into the ideal of "keeping up with The Joneses." This can be felt in corporate life, where the title and the size of your office, or even if you have a window and a designated parking space, means you are successful in your chosen career. It might come from the competitive nature of our upbringing, where quantitative scores in schools, sports, and test scores somehow demonstrate that you are on the right path. And if you are not doing well in those areas, you are somehow a failure of sorts.

All of this makes delaying the gratification of material goods or items that are attached to this status symbol so much more challenging. Personally, I find that if I can surround myself with people who believe in financial independence or who care less about your external status and more about your wellbeing and happiness, then I can withstand the pressures of the outside world and the endless corporate and community comparisons.

That's not to say that I have always been immune to these external pressures. When I was a kid, all I wanted to do was get out of my small town and make it big. Alex P. Keaton from the TV comedy *Family Ties* was my idea of a successful young man. He wore a suit and tie, carried a briefcase, and he always seemed to be working on important things, building his empire. Shortly after graduating from my graduate school with a freshly minted MBA, I was lucky enough to be offered a position within my desired industry, which came with the sort of salary I had never seen before in my life. In fact, by the end of my first year in this new career, I had made more money than I had done in the previous decade! And all those visions of living large took hold. I rented a downtown apartment in one of the largest cities in the USA, completely disregarding the sizable commute and additional city wage tax. My swish new place had its own valets, who would park your car and open to the door for you. They would even greet you by your first and last name. I could take the elevator all the way up and down to my apartment, and I could even take it down to the train station and arrive at the local airport in less than 30 minutes. Incredible—I was really living the life! To complete my city slicker image, I kitted myself out in no end of professional suits and jackets, not forgetting a more modern version of Alex P. Keaton's briefcase, of course.

My next job took me to the mountain states, where I rented a 3,500-square-foot house on a golf course overlooking the mountains. I had a great standard of living and was guided by the Dave Ramsay philosophy of living a debt-free life. I was in complete control of my finances. Life was good, and I had checked all the boxes society had defined as being on the path to success. But why was it that I was still feeling unfulfilled, even empty at times?

You see, up until this point, I hadn't been living according to who I was yet. I hadn't crystallized my own personal *Why.* And it would take a few years to kick in, but once I had a clear vision of where I was headed, the personal sacrifices I would then choose to make to delay my own gratification for something bigger down the road would take hold.

By this time, I was living in beautiful Southern California. My one-bedroom apartment ran just south of $3,000 per month in rent. I had purchased a used luxury car. (It had to be luxury or how could I fit in, right?) I was still debt-free at this time and had even started purchasing a few rental properties, albeit out-of-state back in the Midwest (which is where I am from). I was jumping ahead in the financial freedom plan, but I was starting to scale my strategies before I had fully implemented some fundamental principles of delayed gratification and was increasing my savings to further accelerate the type of net-wealth-building assets that would later completely replace my earned income. Yes, I was doing some of the things you should do, maximizing my retirement, paying off my bad debts, and slowly investing in some assets, but it was going to take me until actual retirement age to get there. Something had to change, and it had to come from within.

MAKING THE CHOICE

When I finally sat down and thought through what I wanted to do in my life—to have more time with my family and friends, to contribute more of my time and skills to initiatives that were more about my own personal values—I knew it was worth making some major changes. Now, I didn't jump ship from my career, but I relocated to a cheaper part of the country, and I even took a step back in title. But the funny thing was my net income increased, given how much I had previously been paying in taxes. These were all really hard decisions and might not be right for you. But you will need to make some fundamental changes if you want to accelerate building your net wealth.

It is hard to make big sacrifices unless you have a clear idea of your *Why* and a vision of a better life for yourself, your family, and friends. Okay, so some people might be happy right where they are—although I don't think they should be. To be honest, I see far too many talented people who perhaps feel they are too far down the road to make changes to truly come into themselves or to do the things they want to do. They have responsibilities that hold them in place. If this is where you find yourself, just start now, and you'll get there. And the sooner you start, the sooner you'll achieve your version of financial freedom.

PLAN, PLAN, PLAN

I cannot emphasize how important it is to draw up a draft of where you are today, knowing where you want to go, and understanding approximately how long it will take for you to get there. This will help you to delay those purchases or impulse buys today. It will program you with an end in sight. Take the time to picture how much net wealth you want to acquire and by how many years. This will help you to create the right amount of additional savings through your net wealth building years, which will create the room you need to pay off your bad debts, to snowball one by one, and then to turn around and increase your emergency fund, level off your retirement, and prepare for the excess discretionary funds you'll need to start investing in assets that will bring your financial plan to life.

Going back to my trusty Excel document, I have a tab that tracks my year-over-year net wealth goals. I have a specific date in my mind that I've highlighted as the time I will become financially free and will be within reach of my *Why*. I started tracking my net wealth in my mid-30s, and I have so far hit my targets every single year. Funny enough, even during the ups and downs of the financial and pandemic crises, I found ways to hit my goals.

You can certainly work with your financial planner, but I suggest that you do some of this planning yourself. Look at your portfolio today, add up your assets (this could include equity on the house, retirement accounts, material items such as a car, etc.), subtract your liabilities (mortgage, student or car loans, credit card debt, etc.), and see where you're at. Then think about where you want to be when you are financially free. What does that number look like? Is it half a million dollars, a million dollars, multi-million dollars? Don't get too hung up in details at this point, as we'll go more into this in the second half of the book. Essentially, the difference between where your net wealth is today and where you want to be is the time you'll need to build wealth. I refer to them as net wealth building years, and each year, you'll set a goal for yourself that builds towards that number.

After this exercise, you might realize you're far behind, but don't worry. I'll help you through each step. The important part of this exercise is to know where you are today, know what level you are reaching for, and to understand how many years you expect it will take for you to get there. This will place an end in sight, a goal post if you will, which will define a timeframe for your financial freedom plan.

4

FOURTH STEP: INCREASING YOUR INCOME TODAY

How many times have you heard someone say that they would start investing and saving if only they had more money? In fact, come to think of it, how many times have you said this to yourself? But is this true? With wage increases stagnant, it is difficult for most people to increase their income. According to the Economic Policy Institute, which tracks nominal wage growth in the USA,[3] we've seen at best a 3% to 4% rise since 2007. So, essentially, in the last 14 years or so, whilst many of you have been at your peak earning years, salary increases have been nominal. And that is frustrating. You might have been in your job for a while, hoping your wage will increase to keep up with your spending. But before getting too despondent, let's look at other ways in which you can increase your income either within your current role or by taking on a second job.

INCREASING INCOME

You might even be able to get the extra income you need by boosting your salary. Negotiate with your current employer to see if you can find additional opportunities to extend your income towards your wealth building assets, such as retirement match contributions, employee stock purchasing plans, or long-term incentives that you can convert in the short term, once vested, and make sure you make the most of your yearly wage and bonus negotiation. I'll also provide you some real-world examples in my own life where I've been able to pick up some side hustles along with ways in which to extend your income from your current employer and job.

So, what is a side hustle? It can be a variety of things, but essentially, it is a part-time gig that you pick up on top of your full-time salaried position to accelerate the additional income you need to save towards the wealth building, creating assets that you'll start to invest. Notice that I used the word "invest" here, not "spend." Part of the problem people typically have with wealth building is that the minute they start to earn more, they begin to spend more too. But this idea is not about working more to spend more. This is about looking for ways to increase your net income today, to complement the increased savings you have created from the previous chapter, to accelerate your net income, and at the end of the month to save towards your net-wealth-creating assets.

Trust me, you'll be cashless for a while during your wealth building years. That's okay though. Soon you'll have plenty of passive income to pay for the things you want, and you'll have all that extra time you've always wanted but never had.

DON'T SPEND MORE

Now, why is it that we struggle to save more when we earn? There's a lot to this question, but one way to look at this phenomenon is through the lens of Cyril Northcote Parkinson, an author and naval historian, who in an article in *The Economist* in 1955, referred to Parkinson's Law, a theory that work expands to fill the time available for its completion. Or the demand for something expands to match its supply. So, the more you have something, the more you consume it. Just think about food, or those after dinner snacks. The more you have the more likely you'll be likely to eat. Eyesight is the same as income and spending: as we increase our net income or take-home pay, we tend to spend to that new income. And it goes on and on throughout our lives.

Another way to explain it is to look at your life over time on a graph, where the X-axis is time, and the Y-axis is money. Now draw two lines, one in green that shows the growth of the income you have been making over time in your life. Then, draw a red line that shows the growth of the expenses you have had over time in your life. Are they separated with the green line above the red? Do they follow each other, almost on top of one another? Or does the red line eventually cross over the green line, literally in the red? It's important to be honest with yourself about where you are today.

Now, if you've followed my recommendations, you should see that red line coming down. And you should hopefully start to see some space between your green and red lines in the future. But it's not enough to invest in passive-income-producing assets that will grow your wealth above what you may have thought possible. You need to also increase that green line, above 3% annually of what you may have been receiving at your current job. The more space you can create between the green line going up and the red line going down, the more it creates a greater opportunity for you in the coming years to invest more and become free.

Do me a favor: go to myssa.gov and look up your year-over-year reported income over your life. Yes, do it! It's incredibly humbling, isn't it? I can see several years where I was making significantly below the poverty line, throughout most of my 20s, in fact. But you know what's funny? I remember having such a great time. I spent a few years as an actor, and I was briefly in a show called *Hang Time,* and I also did some small film and theatre. I loved the creativity of performing and wouldn't change it for the world; however, when my father died, I realized it was time to try and start to earn a "proper living." In a full year of my now "career job," I think I made more than my first 10 years of reported income.

But I wasn't any happier now than I was back then. I might feel a bit more secure in my finances, but my happiness is no greater. Maybe different, as money does provide more options, but I wouldn't trade my previous experiences for anything. It's made me into who I am today. So, print that sucker out and put it in front of you. Circle your best years, even your worst years. Go and put stars around those worst years.

As you add to your income today, by taking on some additional work, and having some much-needed re-negotiations of your contract at work, adding shifts, researching new income streams or benefits at work, and pulling back on your expenses by delaying some gratification, remember that all will be well. You survived back then, and you'll survive now.

Keep your *Why* close to you. Remind yourself every day why you are spending less and working more today to create a free financial future for you and your loved ones. And as you add to your income, either through side hustles or within your current employment, you'll feel a sense of inward satisfaction, knowing that you are tapping into a new you, an entrepreneurial side of your character that can create opportunities today, so you no longer need to rely on an employer or an organization to fund your future. Isn't it good to know that if something were to happen to your regular job, you would have several different streams of income coming in that you could ramp up if you needed to?

Your time will probably be tight during these net-wealth-building years to come, and some of the things you need to do might feel quite humbling, and they might even raise a few eyebrows, but remember that if this path were easy, everyone would be doing the same thing. But most people can't make the necessary sacrifices. Do the extra work today to increase your income, because when you are financially free, you'll have all the time in the world when others may still be stuck in the regular grind. You'll be miles ahead of everyone who has little time to think about what they would do if they had more time. You'll focus on things, how you saved here and there, how you increased your income today by a certain percentage, and how all those extra savings are already going towards your *Why* and not towards some purchase that will add nothing to your net wealth.

THE SIDE HUSTLE

My friends get a kick out of hearing my stories of my side hustles. I remember in my early wealth-building years, I was a full-time executive at a major biopharmaceutical company, and I had a good income. And yet, there I was researching how to become an Uber driver. This is when the app had just started picking up steam, and I had taken Uber and Lyft rides in the past. And of course, I didn't want to admit to too many people that I was entertaining this idea, as if it was some sort of bruise to my ego. I wasn't sure how the whole thing worked anyway. But sure enough, I did my research, and I was on my way to a Sprint store that had the Uber team in the back to inspect my credentials and car. After a few days of a background check, I was approved! Welcome to the team. I received my instructions on how to download the driver app, my stickers, and a step-by-step guide to becoming a legitimate

Uber driver. Looking back, it was all surprisingly seamless, and it was the quickest part-time job I'd ever landed.

Anyway, a few weeks passed, and I still hadn't turned the "on" switch that tells prospective riders you are available. Part of me was terrified of the experience, the other part was the fear that someone I worked with would see me. It was a strange feeling; I'd always had a strong ethic, and we never had any money throughout my childhood, and I was broke until my early 30s, so in a way, I was used to "hustling," whether that was mowing lawns, waiting tables, or painting fences to get by. But another part of me felt a bit uncomfortable about taking on a second job when I had a good salary.

But after thinking through my *Why*, I finally clicked my "on" switch, and my first pick-up was an older gentleman. He sat in the front, and we had great conversation about his service in the military and his years working within the local fire department. I learned more about the local area and even got some real estate tips from this gentleman. Afterward, he dropped me a nice tip and asked me to hang in there, that things would get better for me. I wasn't sure what he meant at the time, but sure enough, after a few more pick-ups, I kept hearing it. "Hang in there." Later, I realized that my riders might have been feeling sorry for me, and that was rather humbling. I would get home and think about folks who drove Uber full-time and wondered if they were hearing the same things.

After a while, I was able to generate a nice chunk of change to drop into my assigned savings that were dedicated towards future investments. Not one dollar went towards a personal expense or payment; these dollars were too important to my net wealth income plan, plus I already had my house in order, and I was living well below my means. My green line, my income line, was going up. For me, the experience was a worthwhile one as it was fully aligned to my *Why*, although I didn't particularly enjoy other people feeling sorry for me. But I think, apart from pride, what might stop others from taking on a second job is that they might not have a strong sense of purpose; perhaps they don't feel the motivation to add more working hours to their day. But I knew exactly why I was doing it: to increase my income to invest in wealth building assets such as property and the market.

FOLLOW YOUR PASSION

Now if becoming an Uber driver isn't top of your list, think of other things you may be passionate about that you could do to make some additional money on the side to help increase your income. One of the things I'm passionate about is politics. My father taught History and American Political System high school classes, and he taught me when I was a sophomore. He used to teach about the Electoral College and how one day we would see a president elected to office who lost the popular vote and yet won the Electoral vote. At the time, it was something that had never occurred in my lifetime, but now, it has happened twice. He's no longer with us, but man, I wish he were alive today!

Anyway, during the 2020 election, I knew I wanted to volunteer and to support our local election board in providing a free and fair electoral process by helping at the local polling stations. I thought I could alleviate the burden that tends to fall on the older generation doing these types of jobs during a global pandemic. It was a ton of training, and I wasn't exactly sure how my skills would be helpful. But sure enough, they found a fit for me. I was an upfront greeter to keep the line moving, I conducted curb side voting services for those unable to go into the polling station themselves, and I was the person who ensured each voter knew how to slot their own ballot into the designated counting machine. I met people who were incredibly passionate about our freedoms and electoral process.

One of the more heartfelt experiences was seeing people vote for the first time, and I can't tell you how incredibly joyous that was. And what's great is that it paid something like $20 per hour, and these were long days. But it meant that more cash could go into those designated savings accounts! So, you never know; get out there and find some opportunities to do the things you would normally enjoy doing anyway—only this time, get paid for them.

INCREASE YOUR SALARY

We have already talked about how to make the most of your benefits package as an employee. A few that I've negotiated are around year-over-year base salary increases, bonuses, long-term incentives, retirement benefits, use of paid time off, and employee stock purchase incentives. I bet there are a few under your nose that you could research too. Now, one simple thing that you can do is to be ready for your performance review each year. It always amazes me that most of my colleagues seem to wait until the last minute to prepare for this. I tend to keep track of my goals and objectives and how I am delivering value to the organization throughout the year, so when it comes time to review my successes against those objectives, they are ready to go, organized and prepared. Don't leave any doubt in your employer's mind of your eligibility for increases in your base pay, promotions, added bonuses, and long-term incentives.

All these things increase your green line of income today over yesterday or the previous year. And you've already taken the steps to redirect those increases to savings towards future investment purchases vs additional expenses that add nothing to your financial freedom. One discovery that was new to me was around employee stock purchase plans. My company offered a 15% discount on up to a certain amount of your annual salary on company stock purchases. I was initially debating this opportunity given how it would make things even tighter than they already were. But after doing the math, I realized that this move would increase my annual net income today, by thousands of dollars, so I went ahead and maxed that out too. I had to make some sacrifices to do so, but after a while, I adjusted again. That might have been one of the best decisions I've made of all the options out there, because it further solidified what I needed and what I no longer required. And it was a discovery of how to increase my net income without any additional work, really. I had to tighten things up a bit, but I didn't have to increase any extra work hours or responsibilities. Personally, I'll take those opportunities any day!

TAX REFUNDS

Finally, I must mention tax refunds. You may not receive one today, but you may start to in the future, especially when changing where your income is coming from. The important thing is to know your tax bracket and to really understand what you are paying to your government. If you usually get some sort of refund, and then one year, you don't, then this should be investigated. Of course, if you do get a tax refund, don't be tempted to spend the money; instead use the entire amount to boost your investment strategy. If you want to be ahead of the game and try to predict any tax refunds, there are various online tax calculators that can help you to do this (such as 1040.com).

I should also add that although I'm not a financial advisor, having real estate investments can impact your overall tax situation in a positive way (at least, it does here in the USA, as I believe it does elsewhere). If you own investment properties, it really does help to bring your overall taxable income down, so that you may be able to reduce your taxes owed even though you are increasing your income. Read *Tax-Free Wealth* by Tim Wheelwright; it really is quite an eye-opener.

I could go on, but I hope some of these ideas inspire you to think of your own ways to increase your net income today. I don't think it matters much exactly what you do, but more how you go about changing your mindset and behavior. Going from just getting through the year and taking a break from the job, to maximizing every opportunity you have today to make more income to go towards things that will make you wealthy, is all worth it. It will test you, and you'll have less time during those wealth-building years, it will humble you too, but all that effort will pay off in the long run.

THE GREEN LINE

Okay, so let's get to it. You've established your *Why,* you've got your house in order, you've reduced your spending, you're living within your means, so what is next? Let's get going on increasing that green income line by finding ways in which you can create greater regular income, either through your existing job, or through a variety of side hustles to generate extra income to save towards future investments. For that regular job, my challenge to you is to target two or three opportunities that you can either discover or negotiate that will create increased net income at the end of the month. For the side hustle, try one or two just to see what's out there; see if it's something you would enjoy doing, perhaps as a complement to what you do for your regular job, or maybe find something completely different that might be fun but pays as well.

If you've already been receiving year-over-year wage increases and/or bonuses and have just been increasing your expenditures or buying things that do not add to your net wealth, then stop. Divert those increases right now into your designated savings account. In fact, I would encourage you to automatically deposit those items right into your net worth accounts rather than into your regular checking and savings account. These increases are going towards specific strategies that we will explore in greater detail throughout the second half of the book.

If you have not received an increase in wages or bonus for a while, I suggest you raise this with your employer, with the evidence to back up your argument that you deserve a raise. If you are not tracking your successes or even the details of value that you are bringing, then I suggest you start doing so now. But also look for opportunities where you can add even greater value to the company, and not just because you want a promotion. You should be compensated for the value you bring to your organization, and if you are not receiving long-term incentives, then I suggest you ask about those too. Of course, long-term incentives may not make a huge difference to your wealth if you plan to retire early, but you need to get into the habit of negotiating for what you deserve.

If you are looking into these types of incentives and just starting out on your financial independence journey, you are likely looking at a window of at least 5, 10, or maybe 15 plus years to create enough net wealth for you to achieve your financial independence. Typically, companies will offer long-term incentives in the form of restricted stock units, which follow the performance of the company and that vest every year. Perhaps you will not collect all your incentives, but you should be eligible for a certain percentage each year. And guess what? Once you've received them, they can all go into more investments.

For specifics on side gigs, things are changing, especially getting through the global pandemic. More people are working remotely, and they want their items delivered. Restaurants are needing to change their infrastructure to deliver restaurant-quality food. Social media, or the age of social influencers, is maturing, and the need for credible and trustworthy people to feature and speak on behalf of products is on the rise. Transportation is evolving, and the concept of owning a car is changing, while reliance on Uber, Lyft, and other services is increasing. Delivering packages via Amazon or through other services is certainly increasing. Your public government institutions are stretched and need your help; they will also pay you for your time and expertise. Just the other day I received a message from the local public health office in need of help with notifying local qualified individuals of their vaccinations. I think I was put on this list because of the work I'd previously done at polling stations. Just put yourself out there and see where there are opportunities for you to pick up some additional income today using the skills you already possess.

Now, these things might seem like a lot or even a bit overwhelming. And they just might be. That's why Steps One and Two in this book are so important to cover first. Life itself is stressful enough. Then layer on a global pandemic, a change in political leadership, working virtually, less enjoyment in the things that you once used to do, uncertainty of what the future may hold, and family demands. You're the one who understands what you can take on now and what you may need more time to do. Be sure to take care of yourself, re-read the first 2 chapters of this book, and do everything advised there first. And if you've completed Step 3 and gotten to Step 4 in this chapter, you'll be in better shape than most of the people around you. They might have the latest car, stylish clothing, and a great trip booked, but they don't have what you have. And that's an increasing green line and a decreasing red line, which will both help to increase your net wealth, rather than creating another useless item taking up space in the garage. You're taking steps towards your freedom, your *Why.* Remind yourself of that. I'm excited for you, because if you've arrived at this point, you're ready for the second half of this book.

Part Two

EXECUTING YOUR NET WEALTH PLAN

5

FIFTH STEP: DEFINING YOUR NET WEALTH PLAN

To recap of the first half of the book, by now you've got a solid sense of your *Why*. Your house is in order, you've grasped the concepts of delayed gratification, made some sacrifices to live below your means, paid off your bad debts such as high interest rate credit cards, car loans, and student debt, and have effectively unhinged as much as you possibly can from the consumption culture that surrounds you.

You're focused on what is important, and you've surrounded yourself with loved ones who understand where you are going and support your plan completely. You have worked through a budget, made some decisions about where you can decrease your expense line (either small things like cutting cable or big things such as moving to a state with lower taxes), you've also taken steps to increase your net income through your regular job, and you have possibly taken on a side gig to further accelerate your cash at the end of the month to save for your future investments. Now, before we jump into the second part of this journey, which is focused on net wealth building and asset creation, let's just take a breath. Look at how far you have come. It might have taken you 6 months or 6 years to get to this point, but you've arrived. You're ahead.

According to NerdWallet's statistics from September 2020[4], the total debt in the USA is roughly around $14.35 trillion, which represents an increase of 2.85% a year. Credit card balances have adjusted down a bit by -6.34%, but still stand at more than $400B, and auto loans are up 3.42% to more than $1.3 trillion, with student loans up 3.47% to more than $1.5 trillion.

I could go on, but let's just take this all in. You are bucking the trend as you have no bad debt, so you have already positioned yourself for success. Yes, you've likely had some failures along the way, but you've had more successes, and more importantly, you have fundamentally changed the way you think about spending and investing. Just look at those debt figures. Congratulations! You deserve a moment to celebrate!

ESTABLISH A TIMEFRAME

But how about we get started on the next phase? Let's get back to your timeframe for achieving financial freedom. Once you reach your goal, this may then involve you walking away from full-time work, or it may just be that you arrive at a place where you feel comfortable in having a Plan B in case your Plan A were to change at any moment. Taking the time to think through how many net wealth building years you will need to arrive at that moment is critical. Knowing your timeframe will help you establish how you are going to get there, what type of passive income channel mix you need to replace your earned income from the full-time job, and, if you choose, to move from your regular income to passive income, to become free without giving your days to someone else or having them determine how you should spend your valuable time.

This is an extremely personal exercise; everyone is in a different place with regards to when they would like to retire and how much they plan to live on, or how much earned income they would like to replace in the future. You can do this exercise on your own, or you can have a financial planner help you with this. There are a variety of different rules of thumb that have been thrown out there, such as the **4% rule**. This idea of withdrawing 4% from a retirement account each year while also maintaining an account balance keeps income flowing throughout your years of non-work is frequently utilized by financial planners and experts. It was later analysed by William Bengen, a financial advisor himself; he discovered no historical case where an individual may run out of funds in less than 33 years given a 4% annual withdrawal from a retirement portfolio. But like any other theory, this isn't fool proof. There are several pitfalls to watch out for. A severe business cycle could erode a higher-risk investment asset. Or, because interest rates now are historically low, current retirees with only "safe bonds" might struggle in maintaining the cash flow desired without investing in riskier assets. Then you also have the human factor, which means, essentially, what if you want to live a little, splurge some in certain years over others? Therefore, I recommend a more diversified asset mix of wealth, including property, market investing, and other asset-building channels such as crowd-lending, syndication, and others.

You need to customize your plan according to where you are in life. What I would suggest is that you go back to your Excel document or to the places where you've documented your goals, your budget (income and expenses), and where you jotted down some initial thoughts on your net wealth goals and net wealth building years. For simplicity, let's say you have roughly $100,000 in net wealth today (maybe just the equity on your home, some retirement savings, and some materials items such as your car, minus any debt owed on those items), and your aim is to simply replace your earned income with passive income from new investments in roughly 10 years.

This is a terrific start to your plan. It's specific, accurate to your current situation, and timebound. But is it realistic? That's up to you. This exercise may involve you asking yourself some tough questions. But for now, let's assume it will be realistic given the earlier steps you've taken from reading this book and your determination to make changes in your investments to accelerate your net wealth towards financial freedom.

ANNUAL GOALS

As part of your plan, you'll want to establish annual goals for your net wealth over time. Each year will have a start and end that will eventually add up to the amount of net wealth generated by new investments over the next 10 years, for example, to completely replace your net income. And guess what? It may not even require becoming a millionaire. Your first few years may start slowly, as you start compounding from your investments to get you to your goals.

Defining net wealth goals, timelines, and a path to get there might seem like an odd ask. In my case, I wasn't ever really asked to do this. From the financial professionals I've worked with to the various books I've read, no one had really broken this down for me. Don't we just save money, put some away for retirement and college for your kids? No. Not if you are planning to become financially free, and certainly not if you are planning to be free in your early life stages. It simply won't be enough. I know it's what everyone else is doing, and that you've made sacrifices already, and your closest friend might have already hit you up with a Bitcoin opportunity or a stock investment that you are tempted to take now. But trust me, you'll need to establish your plan first, so you know where you are going. You'll know if you are falling behind, you'll know where the extra resources are that you're going to be able to draw from, and whether you need to increase your investments or savings, stay the course, or decrease those investments. You'll already have the answers in your plan regarding the type of investments you are looking for. You'll be able to confidently accept or reject an investment idea because you have a plan, a plan that tangibly offers you the opportunity to become financially free within the timeframe that you have defined for yourself.

Let's dig into the specifics with this example. Let's say you're either married with a family or you're single; either way, you have a total household gross income of $100,000. You have made the decision that you'd like to become financially free by replacing your gross earned income of $100,000 with passive income assets that replace that same level of income. You may be in your late 30s and you would maybe like to accomplish this before you turn 50, perhaps even in 10 or less years. Your *Why* is defined, and you've taken the extra steps in the first half of this book to generate some extra savings and have even identified a side hustle that will help contribute to your plan.

Now is the time to lay out what type of asset mix you'll need to increase your net wealth, the timeframe you'll need to get there, and how you'll invest those dollars today to get you to your goals. In this example, we'll also assume that you have a little bit of savings to start investing, but you're not sure what type of assets you should invest in. You already contribute to your company's retirement fund, pay your fair share of taxes, have medical insurance, and are paying into the social security fund. Here, I just need to stress something important: your net wealth plan will not include any entitlements from third-party benefits. **Your plan will be assets that you generate yourself**. Anything above that, such as retirement accounts, pensions, or inheritances are a bonus.

Now, let's revisit the definition of net wealth. It really is very simple: **net wealth is your assets minus your liabilities**. You are starting out with $100,000 in current assets minus any liabilities, and your aim is to build new investments to replace your gross earned income entirely in 10 years. For this example, we are going to look towards investing in some additional real estate, some equity/bonds (such as simple indexes) that are in addition to your retirement account, and perhaps some crowd-lending in the form of backed property as an extra passive income channel. These are just examples to add to your asset mix that will compound your net wealth over the 10 years to help you get to your goal.

If you choose to retire early from your full-time job, you may need to lean on the side hustle for a few years to create some buffer as you transition and focus on maintaining your current lifestyle. For liabilities, you'll likely need to take on some additional debt for the purchase of your real estate investments. Eventually, you can get rid of those liabilities entirely, if it helps you keep your peace of mind, or you might start to consider the idea of leveraging debt as a strategy to build wealth.

What I mean by this specifically is borrowing to invest in real estate and, ultimately, growing your wealth. This, of course, goes against the Dave Ramsey philosophy of being debt-free; but if, for instance, you bought a $100,000 property with a $25,000 deposit and borrowed the rest, you would still then have $75,000 available to invest in the market, which may result in higher returns than having all your money in one property or one asset. **The important part is to start investing**

in assets that will compound over time, to have assets that are well diversified, and to develop several channels to help replace your earned income.

Some people will swear by one kind of investment or the other. I tend to recommend a well-diversified portfolio to balance risk and to allow you to invest in passive income channels with a compound approach. What do I mean by that? Essentially, I'm not looking to time the market with certain purchases of a home or a stock. I'm not going to try to flip a house or to quickly sell a stock (unless it's part of a company stock incentive plan that will go towards my net wealth building plan). What I am trying to do is to establish a consistent set of investments that I can scale during my wealth-building years and replicate year-over-year. This may not be the right strategy for your specific situation, but it has been a formula that I've found builds net wealth consistently.

Now, allow me to dig a bit deeper into the specifics of this example. To establish a set of passive income possibilities to replace your earned income of $100,000 in the next 10 years, let's say, we are going to need 50% from real estate (to buy-and-hold, and not including your own home), 30% in equities/bonds (simple indexes with low expense ratios), perhaps 10% from your side hustle, and 10% from crowd-lending. How the math breaks out is that you are looking to generate $50,000 per year in passive cash flow from your new real estate holdings, $30,000 in passive income from the market index investments, $10,000 from your side hustle, and $10,000 from your new crowd-lending resources.

In my opinion, this ratio of investments guarantees a solid return on building wealth from your invested funds. Real estate has several advantages in building wealth such as cash flow from rent, appreciation, pay-down of leverage, and tax advantages, but it requires a lot more work than investing in the market. Crowd-lending is new and relatively higher-risk, as it is a mix of real estate and the market. At the end of the day, you may need to adjust these ratios to fit your own situation and appetite for risk, but the key message is that you should have a diversified portfolio of passive income channels to protect you from unexpected market events.

At the risk of repeating myself, I am going to mention these ratios again:

- Real Estate—50% passive income
- Market Investments—30% passive income
- Side Hustle—10% passive income
- Crowd-lending—10% passive income

We're going to work on a plan that takes less than 10 years to complete, even if you start from $100,000 or even zero dollars. Your net wealth goals will be strictly tied to these items. You can certainly add in anything on your home, retirement, and emergency savings later; but to keep it simple, let's just look at these key areas of investment for now.

REAL ESTATE

To get to $50,000 in passive positive cash flow in real estate, let's set the plan to invest in 4 single family homes and 2 duplexes, which would give you 8 doors to rent (4 doors from the single-family homes and 4 doors from 2 duplexes) within those 10 years. Let's say that these homes are in Class C and B areas, that they could be within your geographic area or outside of it, and that they give you $500 in positive cash flow per door per month after mortgage, property tax, insurance, and property management expenses. If you have 8 doors bringing in a combined rent of $500 per month in positive cash flow, this gives you a passive monthly income from real estate alone of $4,000 which equates to around $50,000 a year. Now, don't worry here about the details; we'll get there in later chapters. You're just working on the framework of the plan for now. Obviously, you can adjust the numbers to your specific situation and area.

I like real estate first, because it's one of the best ways to increase assets that drive up your net wealth and create passive cash flow for a financially free environment. That's why I'm placing a 50% weight in property investments. But it's not the only one, as I do think diversification is important. And anyone who has invested in real estate knows that it's no walk in the park.

THE MARKET

Let's also look to set up an investment/brokerage account separate from your retirement account (if you have one). This can be done with your financial advisor or with the brokerage that deals with your 401K or pension fund. I don't think it matters too much, given that you are not looking to day trade. That's a different game. One item to look out for is the concept of expense ratios. This is essentially the annual fee as a percentage of your investment that covers the overall funds or investment asset's expenses. This ratio can be found online within the fund's background information, or you can simply ask your financial advisor. To get to 30% replacement of your earned income, you'll need to build up a balance of $300,000 from scratch over the 10 years. This may seem aggressive at first, but let's take a closer look.

I would suggest a broad-based index investment opportunity, perhaps based on the Standard & Poor's Composite Index (or S&P), that averages a return of approximately 8 or 9%, in which you'll contribute monthly over your net wealth building years to allow for compounding. (More on this later.) Contributing $1,500 per month over your net wealth building years, compounding at 8% to 9% over that timeframe from scratch to year 10, will net you close to $300,000. Why $300,000, you might ask? Well, we are looking to compound and to build lasting passive income channels that will not run out. And by building to $300,000, you can safely draw 10% per year just off the interest alone, and you won't have to dip into the principal. This, of course, draws on some growth assumptions, but hopefully you get the idea. This would replace 30% of your earned income today, and this passive income channel will continue to flourish in years to come, even well after your net wealth building years are over.

CROWD-LENDING

You're going to want to build your crowd-lending channel up to $100,000 so you can draw 10% from this base to replace the same proportion of your gross earned income. The thing I like about crowd-lending is that it is purely passive, so you really don't need to do anything once you have made the investment, plus it is still backed by property but doesn't come with the headaches of real estate itself. Again, we will cover this channel in more detail in a bit.

As we establish more detail to your plan, consider whether it is worthwhile to keep your side hustle if you decide to retire from your full-time job, at least in the short term. This would provide you with a buffer so you can continue to build your net wealth. It might also be a good back up plan in case you run into some unexpected expenses when you make the switch. In this example, let's round out to $10,000 per year or less than $1,000 per month from your side gig. So, all in all, the passive income channel mix is 50% from real estate with $50,000 per year in passive income from 8 doors providing $500 a month in cash flow per door; 30% from the market, pulling from a build-up of $300,000 in a broad-based diversified index with low expenses; 10% from crowd-lending real estate which will be built up from a base of $100,000; and the remaining 10% or $10,000 per year will come from your side hustle. This all gets you to $100,000 or more in passive income, replacing your earned income today of $100,000 in 10 years.

Of course, as I have said, this ratio can be tweaked, depending on your own personal circumstances, but I do think this example will provide you with the greatest return on building wealth from your invested funds. Real estate is the best by far but requires more work and a steeper learning curve. Investing in the market is more passive but there is more risk, and less that you can control. Crowd-lending is new and certainly riskier but is the perfect blend of real estate and the market. Whatever you decide, I would stress the importance of having a diversified portfolio of passive income to protect you from various market events.

Now, how do you feel? Does it seem like you have gone from completely unsure to certain? You might be feeling a bit anxious about your ability to do all this, but it is certainly achievable. You already have a framework for looking at investment opportunities and fitting the right pieces together into the plan. You might need to take a little longer to get there, and perhaps you will have to add a few more years to your plan. You might even need to cut back more on your monthly expenses to purchase more investments, or you might decide that you want a different mix of investments; it doesn't matter at this point. **The most important part is to have a plan that's specific and tangible**.

If you were to execute this plan, by following the steps in the first half of this book, you would generate $600,000 in additional net wealth in less than 10 years. You will have the extra savings to invest, and you can also use your bonus or long-term incentives from your employer as well as your tax return or annual incentive and your income from your side hustle to further fund your plan. All this income can be used initially towards the down-payment on your first investment property, for starting that monthly contribution towards the broad-based market index fund with a low expense ratio, or for beginning your first crowd-lending account and figuring out which side gig you'll want once you retire from the full-time one.

STEP BY STEP

If you've finished all the steps in the first half of this book, you're ready to get started. I wish I could have started earlier, but I needed to get my *Why* and my house in order first. I needed to make a few mistakes with my real estate purchases and market understandings, and I needed time to research and discover other passive income channels.

Your plan doesn't have to match the above example but make it real to you. Be honest with yourself. Connect the dots of how you plan to replace your earned income with your chosen investments that are specific to the timeframe you've allocated. Outline what you will invest in. Things may change down the road as you learn more, but have a clear beginning, middle, and end to crossing that goal line.

Breaking down a vision, a mission, or even a complicated thing like financial freedom is not easy. It's not really taught in school or even talked about very much. When a financial planner goes through it with their templates, it might seem too complicated and like something you would normally leave up to the experts. But they might not have the same goals in mind as you do. Many advisors are looking at your income and savings rate and how much you'll need once you hit retirement age.

But that's not your purpose and focus here. You're setting the stage to get free much earlier and faster by using a mix of passive income channels that these traditional advisors may not even have enough expertise in. So, it's up to you. The good thing is that by starting with the end in mind and working backwards, you will realize how to make this vision come true. And that's essentially what we are doing here.

Let's summarize a few of the important steps in this chapter and provide some additional detail to those steps. First, decide on the earned net income that you would like to replace. This number will set the plan in motion. Using the example provided in this book, it's $100,000 per year. And it's okay to start from scratch with zero net wealth. Most people are unable to replace anything given their lifestyle and behavior. But you've done the hard work, made the sacrifices, and generated the necessary additional income to start investing in assets that generate net wealth and passive income, so you can replace your earned income and one day become financially independent.

Next, I suggest thinking through your net wealth building years, or the amount of time it will take for you to build up your passive income channels to replace your earned income. If you're reading this, and you're in your 20s, terrific. You may have less additional savings to draw from, and it may take you a bit more time to compound and invest to build those assets, but the more time you have in front of you, the less disruption you may need to make in some of the earlier steps. If you're in your 40s, you may have more take-home income to invest in those assets, and you may want to be more aggressive with the timeline given your wishes to become financially free while you are in your 40s or early 50s.

I do suggest that you don't include any retirement benefits or entitlements in your net wealth building plan. If you can max out your 401K or pension plans, then terrific. Even better, later, is to compound asset acquisitions into your retirement plan (you'll be an expert by then). Other possible benefits such as Social Security are also things that will only help, but we're not going to lean on them for independence.

The idea of financial freedom is to be able to get after your *Why* much earlier in life, so you can use those productive years when your mind, body, and spirit are at their optimum. And, when you get into those retirement years, and you are eligible to receive those benefits, you'll be prepared to use them more effectively. But your plan is solely reliant on you, and it's better that way.

Once you have your yearly passive income goal, which will replace your yearly earned income, and you have worked out the number of years it will take you to achieve financial freedom, then it is time to set your overall net wealth goal. We discussed how a net wealth building plan is different from the basic concepts of savings and expenses. You want to be thinking of assets (home, real estate, investments, valuable material items) minus your liabilities (mortgages, loans, credit card and student loan debt, etc.). Hopefully by now your existing liabilities have significantly been reduced given the new habits established in the first half of the book. By now, you will have also increased your income either through your full-time job or by taking on a side hustle. All this extra revenue can be used to develop your plan of financial freedom.

Mapping out your net income plan will consist of additional investment assets that will, in turn, provide you with the passive income to replace your earned income. How is this possible? Let's go back to our example, replacing $100,000 in earned income in 10 years of wealth building.

For real estate, you will replace 50% of that earned income with passive income generated by new buy-and-hold real estate investments. You'll plan to purchase 4 single-family homes and 2 duplexes over those 10 years, which will equate to 8 available doors to rent producing $500 in cash flow per door per month, or altogether, roughly $50,000 a year. Let's say all 6 properties would cost $700,000 to purchase over those 10 years. And let's assume that during your net wealth building years, you put down $155,000 in total down payments to acquire and rent them. Your net wealth for those properties will be around $200,000 (we'll assume appreciation in value over time and a reduction in liabilities of the mortgage) at the end of your 10-year plan.

For the new market or index investments, you're looking to build up $300,000 from scratch and to draw 10%, or $30,000 per year, to replace 30% of your earned income. If you are looking at 10 years of net wealth building ahead of you, with a $1,000 initial deposit, and committing to investing $1,500 per month over that timeframe, compounding at 9% return over those 10 years, this will result in approximately $300,000 in new wealth. Again, you can adjust the figures for your timeframe, including what you feel comfortable calculating as a return, and what you can realistically contribute monthly. But, if you follow this example, you'll have $300,000 in net wealth at the end of 10 years, adding to your $200,000 in net wealth from real estate, giving you close to half a million dollars in new net wealth in a 10-year timeframe.

For your third passive income channel, you'll build up your crowd-lending backed by real estate properties from scratch to $100,000 over that same timeframe. This will require an initial investment of $1,000, plus a $500 per month contribution, at roughly 8% interest over those 10 years, and it will get you approximately $100,000 in that time. Like your market investment, you'll have a good base to draw 10% from without dipping into the principal.

This new $100,000 passive income channel will also add to your total new net wealth of half a million dollars, which will then total $600,000 over those 10 years. The remaining 10% of passive income you need to replace your earned income will come from your part-time work, which you'll plan to keep in the short term.

MORE DETAIL

Now that you have a plan to replace 100% of your earned income with passive income in the next 10 years, resulting in up to $600,000 of net wealth, let us look at your plan on a yearly basis. To achieve your goal, you'll need to buy 1 investment property every other year, along with consistent investments in the new market index account and crowd-lending channels every month. This probably seems like a lot of additional money and savings that you'll need to generate. It certainly won't be easy but stay with me. That's why the first half of the book was so important. The new way in which you approach saving and spending will mean that you will undoubtedly have extra savings and income to invest in your plan.

To hit these net wealth numbers, you'll need to plan on investing in a property every other year (a contribution of $15,000 each year), while also consistently investing in the market index fund (a contribution of $16,800 each year) and crowd-funding investment opportunities (a contribution of $6,000 each year), all of which adds up to $37,800 in investments. Now, you might be thinking that isn't possible. So, I would urge you to go back through the first half of the book and really challenge yourself. If you need to make some adjustments, that's okay.

Maybe replacing all your earned income in 10 years is not the goal; perhaps it's 80% of your earned income in 15 years. Find what works for you. But you might be thinking, wait, making $37,800 a year over 10 years only adds up to $378,000 in additional net wealth. So, where did that figure of $600,000 come from? Well, the beauty of this plan is that it's not only diversified, but it will also compound your net wealth year-over-year, both during your net wealth building years and well beyond. Technically, you will be almost doubling your net wealth over what you put in as the principal. Now we can have your money work for you! This is where things get exciting.

But let's not get ahead of ourselves. Complete your plan, lay out your expected additional net wealth year-over-year in those 10 years until it adds up to $600,000. We'll get more into diversification and compound principles when we break down even further how we make this plan come to life. I have found other books on wealth building to be a bit too theoretical and not practical enough. My hope is to provide you some basic principles in building and executing the plan to achieve your goals. You'll have a map of year-over-year growth against that $600,000 net wealth additional accumulation if you are following something like the example in this book. You'll have some ups and downs, but you'll see progress. And this progress will only further fuel your desire to get there, to cross that finish line, and to ultimately get your time back. I am excited for you! Let's get started.

6

SIXTH STEP: BUILDING YOUR PASSIVE INCOME

Just mentioning the term "real estate investor" might send a chill down your spine. For those who are in the industry, it's just an ordinary day in a chaotic paradise. For others, it's a complete mess. We all know people in our immediate family who have taken a crack at it. It's usually an uncle or a brother who is trying to get you involved in a new real estate opportunity.

When I was growing up, the concept was introduced to me by my father, who was a high school teacher. He had bought a second home in a different part of the small town where I grew up. I believe it was because a good friend of his had talked him into it. I can recall that home vividly, as he hired me to work on it over a few summers. I remember painting the outside of the house, updating the landscape, and overall, just giving it a good clean-up, and I was thrilled when my father increased my hourly rate from $2.40 per hour to $4.

After my father died, and I was putting his affairs in order, I discovered that he had rented that house for less than the monthly mortgage payment. Not surprisingly, his previous tenants had nothing but good things to say about him. Pops was a terrific man, who instilled in me healthy discipline and accountability. But as a real estate investor, he clearly didn't know what he was doing. I don't think he had that overall plan on what he was trying to do, and I so wish he was alive today, as I have a million different ideas about what he could have done with that house, and I would have really enjoyed helping him to make it a profitable investment.

Despite this cautionary tale, real estate, in my opinion when done right, is an incredible net wealth creation vehicle, especially if it's not your own home we are talking about. It's no doubt challenging, and those of us who have completed multiple deals know that it can really put you through the ringer. And this is on top of the daily stress of having that regular job and just trying to live in today's world. There's no doubt there will be challenges, but when it comes to sustainable wealth creation, it's worth the lessons, the ups and downs. That's why we are starting here first with real estate in the net wealth building plan and investing 50% of our efforts (based on the example in this book on our path towards financial freedom).

FEEL THE FEAR

But before we go on, I'll admit knowing how and where to invest in real estate can be overwhelming. There are wholesalers, house flippers, vacation and Airbnb opportunities, things called REITs (or real estate investment trusts), syndications, online crowd-lending sites, and the traditional buy-and-hold investment opportunities. This is just a list off the top of my head, and I'm sure I'm missing a slew of other options. It's easy to freeze and to get lost in analysis paralysis. In other words, the fear of losing out or making a mistake or failing at something new grips potential investors before they even get started.

Despite all the hard work you have already put in to get to this stage, you might feel afraid to put money into an investment you are not as familiar with as part of your savings. But you must know that just saving will not get you to your goal. At the expected rate of future inflation, savings rates won't be enough to keep up with the loss of dollar value, let alone achieve your financial freedom plan. So, let's embrace the fear; let it energize you into putting in the work on that next investment when the time is right and it's a good fit with your plan. We've identified your *Why* and you have outlined your net wealth plan, so you know what kind of real estate investor you want to become, and the type of assets you are looking for. You've stripped away as much uncertainty as you possibly can. You're ready, and if you need more information, carry on reading in this book, because there's more!

So, "buy-and-hold"—what does that mean anyway? Well, it means literally that. You're looking to buy and to hold properties as part of your portfolio that will help to build your net wealth. It is sort of like Monopoly (which I love by the way, and the app is great too). Now, you don't necessarily need to hold onto a particular property forever, but your plan is to have a solid mix of properties within your portfolio that make up your net wealth to help support the passive income you are looking to use to replace your earned income. You are also looking to build a foundation to grow further; perhaps you can amass a large set of residential properties well past your initial net wealth plan. Or you can start fixing and flipping homes for that additional income, to help you to further invest in the portfolio of assets that will continue to build your overall net wealth.

But, for the purposes of the plan outlined in this book, what I would suggest as a good starting point is a buy-and-hold strategy. It doesn't require as much up-front capital, although this will depend on your location or country of course. In many parts of the USA, including the Midwest, the South, and the Southeast, it really is possible to buy a decent residential property for between $100,000 and $150,000.

Also, there are several advantages to this strategy, one of which are tax deductions you are eligible for as a rental property owner, which in the USA includes payments towards mortgage interest, property tax, insurance, property management fees, repairs, and advertising. All these count as business expenses and so can be used to reduce your tax liability. You can also use the depreciation of that property over time as an expense. Appreciation, or the increase in value of the properties you own over time, builds equity as you pay down your mortgages from the rental payments you receive. I am certainly not a tax attorney, and I would suggest you work with a qualified expert who understands the nuances of having an earned income whilst being a passive income builder.

BUY-AND-HOLD

Buy-and-hold investments have many advantages that you'll start to realize as you build wealth. Since making my own property purchases, I have completely changed the way I view real estate today. It's hard for me to drive through a neighborhood these days without being distracted by visions of what I could do to improve the community, the properties, and the possible tenants that my company would service. Before my financial freedom plan kicked in, I just sort of thought of real estate as that one big purchase you made in your life. Now, this does mean you are technically going to become a landlord, but there are different ways of managing rental properties. I have friends who love this kind of stuff. They enjoy being involved in all the detail and fixing things, getting into the remodelling, and buying new sprinkling systems. For me, that's what either a property management agent or a trustworthy repair maintenance professional is for. Some landlords love interacting with tenants, and they get a kick out of marketing their properties, drawing up leases, and setting up accounting systems. I don't like to get that involved, and I prefer to hire professionals to attract reliable tenants. But it's up to you how hands-on you want to be with the various properties in your portfolio.

It's a good idea to start by working with a reputable property management company, as this can be a good way to learn how to optimize a self-managed property. I do suggest having at least one under your management in the early term of your wealth building plan, so you can experience the entire process. This may include deal evaluation, financing, closing, marketing, securing tenants, rent, and maintenance/repairs as well as covering any vacancy, upkeep, and future repairs. This will be a healthy education for you in your learning as a real estate investor.

I still self-manage some of the properties in my portfolio today. However, I do suggest you keep an eye on your overall net wealth plan and how much time you want to or can dedicate to this passive income channel. If you are looking at scaling to at least 6 properties in 10 years, plus building a few more channels, all while holding down your full-town job and maybe even a side gig (if you're following the example in the book), that's a lot, and you're going to need to be very efficient with your time. And there are partnerships that you can develop and teams that you can put together that will help take on many of these responsibilities. Most of my properties are managed by reputable companies, and this allows me to focus on the financing and asset acquisition, all while providing affordable and desirable locations to call home for my tenants.

As promised, I want to make sure that I not only provide you with the strategies and philosophies that will help you to work towards financial independence but also some tangible real-world examples to back them up. Many of these examples are properties that I have bought. They may not be right for you, but I hope they will help to connect the dots so that you can create your own wealth building opportunities.

BUILDING WEALTH

One of the challenges of building wealth is that it's not really taught in our schools, or if it is, then it is taught by people who haven't necessarily gone through the steps themselves. It's also hard to see wealth generation in real life. There are plenty of examples of "rich people" around with their expensive homes and various cars. But these individuals aren't necessarily wealthy, as in many cases, aside from the trappings of their lifestyle, they might not have much in real assets. They're all caught up in the consumption game and define success from an exterior perspective.

So, let's try and paint a picture of what wealth building today mighty look like. We will use the example in Chapter 5, where we laid out a plan to replace your $100,000 earned income with $100,000 in passive income. Within this example, you are looking to build real estate assets in the form of rental properties, with a specific buy-and-hold strategy that accumulates 6 properties, adding up to 8 doors. You are looking to establish long-term rentals, with quality repairs and infrastructure, not necessarily in the most expensive neighborhoods, but within an affordable range to purchase and to rent.

Let's say you are looking to buy 4 single family homes and 2 duplexes over the range of the 10-year net wealth building timeframe we outlined earlier. The value of these properties will come to roughly $700,000, and you will be putting $155,000 of initial equity into these purchases. This is based on 20% up-front payments for the single-family homes, and 25% for the duplexes. Keep in mind that you're not planning to buy all this property at once, but instead, you're looking to spread out these purchases over your 10-year net wealth building period. If executed correctly, this should ultimately translate to $500 per month per door of cash flow, and ultimately, 50% of your passive income will come from real estate holdings.

Once it is written down, is so important to stick to your plan. Without it, you'll likely be running around in various directions, sometimes making investment decisions without a clear line of your endgame. Take the time to know where you are going, not just in your overall net wealth plan, but specifically within each passive income channel. It'll make the actual purchasing of the properties seem relatively easy, as you've already done your research and ensured each investment is right for your plan.

THE FIRST PROPERTY

So, let's get started with that first property. Let's say you're set on a single-family rental house, one that you will either self-manage or eventually turn over to a property management company. Your target purchase is around $100,000 with recent repairs completed on key items such as roofs, heating and cooling systems, and other expensive items that can rack up costs in your early years as an investor. **You're looking for areas where rent demand is solid and there are good employment, attractive schools, and low crime rates.** Properties that meet these criteria might come from a real estate agent who specializes in working with investors, a local association focused on real estate investing, or even trusted turnkey operators, that is, companies that buy, refurbish, and then sell good investment properties.

It really depends on your level of experience and how much you want to get involved. If you're someone who wants to get your hands dirty, then think about getting a real estate licence and finding your own investment properties. If you're more of the hands-off type, perhaps working with a trusted turnkey operator is the way to go, using a back-end property management firm. Personally, I am not really interested in becoming a real estate broker, a construction expert, or even a guru in rehabbing and lending. I am looking for passive income with a view to compounding to 6 properties that are well diversified and supported to achieve my net worth goals. I don't want to spend my time once I'm independent focused on the daily nitty gritty of just real estate.

So, let's say working with a local real estate agent and property management firm is where we start. For lending, you're looking for traditional residential lending, and I would suggest looking for lenders that again specialize in working with real estate investors, those that understand what you are trying to do. Your trusted local bank may not be the way to go. In fact, I prefer using national lenders that have a reputation for working closely with real estate investors that purchase in multiple locations at a high level throughout the year. It's just easier in terms of the paperwork and turnaround. They'll also speak to you in terms of numbers that you are looking for, how much you are looking to put down, and what you want to have as a desirable interest loan. Ultimately, you will be treated as an investor rather than a homeowner.

If your house is in order, and you are increasing your savings, and you are careful to avoid some of the most expensive neighborhoods to invest in, you should be able to collect the financing you need to scale to these 6 properties. You may even be able to go a bit further in total lending, and perhaps you may need to go a bit less. That's okay; the great thing is you can always adjust within your channel to fit the plan. For example, if you can only purchase 4 investment properties with 6 doors, don't worry. You'll just need to bring in more cash flow per door. If you can do more, then great; or perhaps you can do less cash flow per door. Some of the books I've been reading state that you need 30 doors to get to $5,000 per month in free cash flow. That might be true in certain situations or locations, but for someone who is just starting out in building assets with a full-time job, that sounds like a daunting task. And from my own experience, I can say that I think it's unnecessary, although I do plan to go much further than 30 properties in total, given my growth and experience.

But again, keep it simple, stick to the plan, and tweak here and there to suit your own situation. What I'm hoping is that this plan will show you that you don't have to be a millionaire or to have a million bucks to start as an investor. You don't need any of those things, and if you've followed the earlier steps, you have everything you need to get started.

CRUNCH THE NUMBERS

Next, let's start analysing some potential investments for practice. I use a few methods in evaluating various properties. The one I'm most comfortable with is cash on cash return, which measures your return on the actual cash you have invested. I like this method, which can also be used for stocks, bonds, or index funds. There are some fantastic tools online to help you calculate this return; Bigger Pockets has a great resource, where you can plug in the listing price, financing, rental income, property taxes, insurance over variable costs such as utilities, repairs, possible vacancy time, and management. Don't worry about extensive research at this stage; just start by getting some potential properties to use as examples and get used to plugging in the numbers.

I read somewhere that you should research 100 properties before you purchase even your first one. This might be a good idea, as you're building towards your down payment. Some important numbers to look for are actual rental prices over the list price, ensuring that all the expensive items of a home have been taken care of, or if not, then building that into the cost of repairs. Know your lending criteria in advance and doing your research on the property tax is important too, as well as looking closely at potential insurance and variable costs. I tend to list each item fully priced, without much wiggle room, and in many cases increase that price a bit to hedge on anything I may have missed in the initial evaluation.

What I like to look for is an investment that will produce something in the range of 12% to 18% cash on cash return, which hopefully will yield $300 to $400 in cash flow per month. These numbers may be challenging to achieve where you live, but you could always consider investing elsewhere. In these early stages of wealth building, you are looking for good cash flow with minimal expenses, so that you can build your asset portfolio quickly.

Now, it's important to realize that with your first purchase you might not get $500 per month right out of the gate, and that is okay; you'll get there over time. Remember, this is your first purchase, and you've got several years in front of you in which you'll be renting this property, paying down the mortgage, and benefiting from the appreciation in value and future rents.

HAVE INTEGRITY

When you're ready to pull the trigger, I suggest you also look at the type of investor you want to become. Ideally, you should want to build a reputation as someone who is trustworthy, who knows where they are going and what they are trying to do. Too many other investors out there may be looking to lowball, or to pressure the seller, and maybe those are strategies that are recommended by other professionals. But for me, it's about your *Why*, and if part of your *Why* is to provide a service to others, then make sure you carry that forward in your asset creation. Try to be an investor with an honest reputation who owns attractive, affordable properties that are well managed and well financed .

Once you have made your first purchase, you'll want to work through any inspections, appraisals, and repairs that you need. When it comes to marketing your rental property, there is no need to wait around; instead, work with your agent and/or property management firm to establish a good marketing plan, get decent photos and descriptions, and decide on the rental prices you're looking for, who's handling the applications, and any other incentives that will help you secure the right tenant. There are several things that you'll need to do when it comes to finding appropriate tenant care, which is why working with a property management firm might be a good idea at first. Okay, so you'll be giving up a percentage of the rent, but you'll learn so much, and this will eventually help you to self-manage further properties, if that is what you choose to do.

Once you have secured your first tenant, hopefully someone who will be with you for some time, you'll want to have good systems in place to address maintenance requests and collect rent. I prefer online payments, and there are several that are out there if you are self-managing (for example, Apartments.com). If you're using a property management firm, then they'll address these things. But keep an eye on them, and make sure they are delivering on their agreements and taking care of your properties and your tenants. You are in charge here, and no one will care more for your investments than you.

Now, without going through the entire 6 properties, this is a framework that you can scale and replicate for each one and with each step of the process, perfect your approach. You'll discover how to source property deals with greater efficiency, you'll have a good understanding of what your lender needs from you and how to negotiate deals that fit into what you are doing, and you'll start to understand the marketing side of things as well as what to look for in property management and how to build good stewardship of your assets. Once you've made that first purchase, you'll need to quickly replenish those dedicated savings accounts towards your next property purchase, all while building those other channels. But you'll get used to it, you'll discover ways in which you can automate many of the deposits each month, and you'll see your net wealth start to compound and come to life.

Getting into real estate can be overwhelming, and it might seem like too much at first, but I cannot stress this enough: **long-term buy-and-hold investing in real estate is a terrific way to build your net wealth and generate passive income**, and one that will continue to compound over time with good management and professionalism.

As I have said before, creating your own property portfolio will also profoundly change the way you look at real estate. Today, I live in a 3-bedroom town house in an accelerating growth area where people are mainly retiring. Demand far outweighs supply. And if you knew me, you'd be a bit puzzled by this decision. Why would I not choose to live right near downtown, or just above the good restaurants? It's not what I'm looking for, at least not right now. I want to reduce my expenses significantly and appreciate all my properties, including the one I live in today, which is up substantially from when I purchased it a few years ago.

So, don't be intimidated; my hope is that this book helps you get organized and to get after it. Next, we review some of the new habits you'll want to build as a real estate investor.

USEFUL HABITS

First, remember that **you've got time**. You don't need to purchase 6 properties and have 8 doors fully rented within 12 months. In fact, you can take the entire first year to search, discover, finance, negotiate, purchase and repair, market and lease your first property. You're going to make mistakes, but just make sure you learn from them, so that your next purchase is even more optimal than the previous one. After my first few investments, I found that my cash on cash return continued to improve on each sequential purchase. A little bit of "right time, right place," but perhaps it was more a case of me being prepared when those opportunities presented themselves. So, don't feel as if you need to rush. What you must do is to make sure your finances are in order; be sure you have built up enough savings for that down payment (20% for that single family home) along with closing costs and some extra for unexpected expenses that may arise.

And while you are waiting for your first investment opportunity to arise, pull together a team comprised of your lender, a real estate agent, a property management firm, and/or contractors, and make sure you have insurance and legal support in place. When I'm preparing for my next purchase, I let the people who will be working with me on the investment know that I am prepared to make a purchase in the next few months, and that I have everything in order.

Second, start establishing a habit of **looking at deals**. You can even practise by looking at the Multiple Listing Service (MLS) or other property listings, depending on which country you live in. Ask your agent to start sending you single family homes for investors in good rent areas with positive appreciation and within the price range you are looking for. Start evaluating the MLS information, get used to plugging in the numbers to calculate your cash-on-cash return-on-investment (ROI). Eventually, you'll know exactly what you are looking for.

For example, if you want to quickly get to $400 per month cash flow out of the gate, building towards that $500 per month cash flow in a few years, with a 15-16% cash-on-cash ratio for a $100,000 purchase, you'll likely need a home that rents at $1,000 per month with property tax and insurance around $1,200 per year, minimal repairs needed, standard assumed vacancy rates, and normal utility and property management expenses.

If it's a local investment, get in there and look around. It's a lot different from purchasing your own home. You're looking at the building as an investor, and the questions you need to ask yourself will be a bit different. For instance, does this property appeal to the type of tenant who will likely want to rent from you? If you're out of state, be sure you understand the area and have trusted people on the ground who know exactly what you are looking for. And when you're ready, jump in, and give yourself the opportunity to learn and grow.

Third, rely on your **professional team** to help you negotiate and secure the deal that you've researched. I may run an initial analysis. You will get better at it, and you'll start to learn where to give and take in the negotiation. Ensure that the roof, heating and air conditioning systems, flooring, lighting, kitchen, appliances, plumbing, bathroom, windows, and exterior are all in good shape. You can purchase a depressed property and build it up. Some investors do this to purchase the property, which they then repair and rent out only to refinance it later. It's a great strategy, one of which, if you have the time and resources, might be right for you. If not, that's okay too; you can still find good properties that are ready to rent straightaway to get the cash flow coming in during that first month of rent. Ideally, you want to have a house rented as you close the deal, so don't sit back on marketing your property. Get your management firm to do this as a matter of urgency.

Finally, make sure you have **systems in place** to collect your rent, pay your mortgage, and to address any property management needs. Have some automated systems set up so this portion of your net wealth building plan doesn't completely consume nor deplete your energy.

Before we move on, let's summarise what you need to do before buying your first investment property:

- Do your research.
- Start looking at deals.
- Get a professional team in place.
- Create systems for rent and mortgage payments.
- Enjoy the ride!

Trust me: it can be exciting to see your plan coming to life, as the concept of passive income becomes a reality. You are now working towards a life where you are in the driver's seat, and you aren't tied to a company or a 9-to-5 job. This will be a life where you can come fully into your own as an entrepreneur or a business owner or whatever else you choose to be. Keep this in mind as you scale as a real estate investor and make use of any of the skills you have acquired in your regular job to create your net wealth.

Being a real estate investor is very much about working with others. It's another way in which you can fully come into the vision for yourself, and you might just discover the real you during this process!

7

SEVENTH STEP: ADDING MORE CHANNELS

One of my first memories of understanding the concept of "the market," or stocks, bonds, and mutual and index funds, was watching my mother pace in front of the television (before there were remote controls) and cheer on a ticker that would run across the screen. I had no idea what was going on, but apparently, we had placed investments on some firms which we were hoping would make us wealthy. Or, at least that was what was going on inside my head as I sat at home in our small town in the Midwest. We might have made a bit here and there, but it didn't seem to make much of a difference to our family's income or wealth.

The idea that you can invest in some big company and have them pay you something in return, without having to go out and cut the grass or serve pizzas for 8 hours straight, seemed exciting to me. It wasn't, though, until my grandfather sat me down and started to explain how the market worked, the differences between company stocks and bonds, and the different kinds of returns to calculate, and how having a mix of everything seemed like a good way to "play it safe" and make some money in the future. But, as much as the diversification concept was making sense at that time, what was still missing for me in those early years was the idea behind compounding (which we touched on in Chapter 4).

COMPOUNDING

You see, no one ever broke this concept down for me. I'm desperately trying to recall if this was taught in school, college, or even graduate school, and I really don't think it was. In fact, I didn't start to understand the concept of compounding until I saw it working for myself. I stumbled upon it when I started investing in my company's 401K, the equivalent of a retirement fund. At that time, I really didn't want to put away money from my pay into an investment account that I wouldn't be able to touch until I was into my 60s. That seemed like forever, and I had important financial needs, such as paying off student debt and buying all the stuff that tends to consume someone who has some money on their hands.

But there was this company match that caught my attention. In other words, my company would pay a 6% monthly match to whatever I contributed up to an allowable amount for the year. That seemed like free money or at least a way to increase my net income or salary. That was enough for me to start contributing towards this idea of retirement money.

It wasn't until I hit my mid-30s, when I really started to see the concept of compounding kick in, however. I noticed that the 12% return per year was really starting to make a difference on my principal. By that time, I had something like $100,000 in my 401K, and I was contributing on a biweekly basis out of my paycheck, which was going directly into my investment account. It was a good year to get to that 12% return, but when I noticed that my account had jumped to $125,000, I was sort of excited and confused at the same time. Doing the quick math in my head, I worked out I was paying in $1,000 a month with my company's match, or $12,000 for the year, and yet I had made more in compound interest of $13,000 than I had personally contributed to the fund. **To my amazement, I discovered that compounding interest, which is essentially interest on your deposits** and **on your accumulated interest on those deposits, meant that you could make more money than perhaps you invested over time.** And that to me felt like nothing short of magic.

That's when things started to click, and I realized that by expanding my window of income, reducing my expenses, and compounding by investing into the market early and on a regular basis, I could really begin to increase my net worth. The only frustrating part of it all was knowing how much more I could have achieved if I'd started when I was younger! But as I've already mentioned, finance still isn't part of the school curriculum; however, in my opinion, the principles of managing money and making it work for you should be available to all students. Because if you have control over your finances, you can then make real all the visions and plans you have for your life. I think all young individuals should at least be taught the fundamentals of budgeting, delayed gratification, and compound interest, as well as learning how to increase your income, live below your means, and execute a net wealth plan.

START INVESTING

Now, getting back to the plan, we are going to set up a separate account from your retirement account, if you have one. Keep that 401K, your

IRA, and your Roth IRA going. These are tax-free retirement accounts, with the first being a vehicle for tax-free deposits (although you are taxed on funds when you withdraw them), whilst with the second, you are taxed as you deposit but then the funds are tax-free. Obviously, these are constructs developed in the USA, but similar vehicles will be available in other countries.

The behaviors you put into building this second passive income channel will be like those you have used to put towards your retirement account. If you have not started a retirement account yet, please review the first half of the book. Now, let's get started on your investment journey by opening a separate account. It could be with the same investment firm where you have your retirement accounts. There's no need to complicate things, and I would suggest looking into simple index or ETF (exchange traded funds)investments with low expense ratios that have had reliable returns year-over-year. For those of you who are unfamiliar with this product, it is bundle of investments in various stocks and bonds that can be purchased in a single transaction. They are a great way of diversifying whilst keeping your investments relatively uncomplicated.

If you are following the example in this book, the goal is to produce $300,000 in net wealth from investments within 10 years, after which, you'll be able to draw 10% a year, which will replace almost a third of your earned income. What you are aiming for, once you are financially free, is to have 50% of your annual passive income coming in from real estate and 30% from the market. With an initial deposit of $1,000 in a broad index/ETF fund with low expense ratios, while contributing $1,500 per month over the next 10 years at 9% interest compounded, you'll achieve this goal.

Now, some of you may be reading this and thinking, where do I find $1,500 per month on top of saving for those real estate properties?

It's a good question, and your plan can be adjusted for your personal situation, but let's still try to make it work. If you have a household income of $100,000, and you've taken the steps to maximize your income, reduce your expenses, and pay off unnecessary or unproductive debt and have taken up a side hustle, you can do this. If you're not there yet, go back to the earlier chapters in this book.

If you are there, I would suggest you have built up $30,000 per year to invest in the first passive income channel of savings towards your real estate purchases and your second passive income channel in monthly contributions towards your broad-based market index fund over those 10 years of wealth building. Year-over-year, it might fluctuate depending on when you purchase those real estate assets (in the example it will be 6 properties), but your contributions towards your market index will be the same each month.

YOU CAN DO THIS!

Now, remember, you've taken steps to pull in your bonus, long-term incentives, and employee stock purchase plans from your regular job; you've negotiated for increased yearly salary increases and possible promotions; you've reduced your monthly expenses, pivoted your debt payments into savings towards your assets, and added a side hustle. Plus, you'll have cash flow coming in from your real estate purchases that will also start to compound and will help contribute to the plan. Those first few years will be tight, no doubt about it. I did mention that you would need to make some changes to make this happen, but this is doable and will get easier with time.

Do you need to make some drastic changes, such as moving completely from a high-tax state to a low-tax one, going without a car, or without purchasing a new one for 10 years, and not making any large purchases for some time? Perhaps. It all depends on your goals, so go back to your plan to review them. You may need to sacrifice more if you want to increase your net wealth and shorten the length of time it will take for you to be financially free. You may lengthen your time and adjust the amount of net wealth you are aiming for, knowing that you plan to work part-time; or freelancing may buy you more time to build out your plan. It's completely customizable towards your own personal situation. My hope is that you start to see how the mix of real estate and market investments as 2 passive income channels really start kicking in and contributing towards replacing your earned income.

If you started from zero, by following the example in this book, you'll have effectively replaced 80% of your earned income, producing $80,000 per year in passive income, all while keeping your day job. And that total is more than twice the average earned income of in the USA in 2019. You can do this, and you don't have to necessarily become a millionaire to do so. In fact, with this example, at the end of 10 years, with your real estate and your market investments, you'll have effectively generated $500,000 in net wealth.

Eventually, if you keep going, paying off those mortgages on your real estate investments, buying more properties, and contributing into your market channel, you will cross that finish line entirely. Remember, this is just with the 2 additional channels you've added (we will discuss more ideas later) plus any retirement or other income you may have. There are several ways to get there, but the important part is to start investing, in more than one channel, to further diversify your income streams.

INVESTING IN THE MARKET

It can be challenging to get your head around the market if you have never invested before. There are so many ways to invest, even more so than in real estate, in my opinion, and it can be overwhelming. I will say that most of my conversations with family and friends who come to me to try and understand what I'm doing center on questions that may involve a particular stock or sector of the economy. When I offer advice, it depends on the strategies they are looking to deploy. It goes back to that person's *Why.*

If you're looking to make a quick return, to invest in other tangible items, and you need the resources from that return quickly, then that is a different strategy. If your *Why* is to place some big bets in the hopes of turning around some big returns, that's also a different strategy. The one we are laying out here is not to try and make a quick buck, or necessarily to replace your earned income job with a day-trading strategy that you hear about on CNBC. If that's where your passion is, then this part of the book might be a bit boring for you.

As a working professional who is looking to free up more time to connect to their sense of purpose, to leave the rat race, and who would like to add an investment channel with the market to turn into passive income, this game is about compounding, based on simple diversified assets that produce reliable and consistent returns, have low expenses, and allow for future cash flows to replace a portion of your earned income. That's really it. It will be a slower process than day traders, perhaps a bit less exciting one. But it requires discipline, a few key decisions up front, but it will not be too complicated or require a lot of your time once things are set up.

Your time is precious during your net wealth building years, even more so given the balance of executing this plan all while holding a full-time job. You'll also want to keep it simple, given the balance you'll have in building your other channels in real estate buy-and-hold strategies, and perhaps some additional ones in crowd-lending, along with a possible side hustle.

DON'T DELAY

Before we go on, I really want to make this point. The younger you are when you start investing, the more likely you are to create greater levels of net worth. So, encourage your children to start investing as soon as they are legally able to do so. In the meantime, why not open custodial accounts for them whereby you can invest for them until they can take ownership? I have already got my girlfriend's teenage daughters invested in their custodial Roth IRAs, and I am encouraging my niece and nephew and anyone else who's interested in the subject to save as early as possible.

Making investments as early as you can and keeping up with regular contributions is essential if you want your plan to be a success. Have your net wealth plan on hand. In the previous example, we are looking at replacing 30% of our $100,000 earned income salary with an investment in the market to produce a second passive income channel. There are lots of different ways of going about achieving this, but for this example, we want to build up a nice principal of $300,000 that we can rely on to draw $30,000 a year (30% of your passive income) to add into the mix of your contributions to real estate and other channels. I know $300,000 sounds like a lot, and you may need more or less than this amount, depending on your plan. If you have taken all the steps recommended in the first half of this book, you should most certainly be able to do this.

So, how do we get to $300,000 in 10 years? Well, first, do an internet search on something called a **compound interest calculator**; when you find one, pull it up in a browser and start to plug in some numbers that involve an initial deposit of $1,000, with monthly contributions of $1,500 per month at a 9% interest rate, and this will get you close to that $300,000. Feel free to adjust on your understanding of the market. What I like about this strategy is that it's less about trying to time the market or "play the game." This is about consistent behaviors of investing. Just as you are doing with your real estate purchase strategy, where you are looking to consistently add to your net wealth by buying rental properties, here you are investing in well diversified assets with low expense ratios, which you will contribute to every month.

And what may make this a bit easier for you is that once you've set up your individual brokerage account and selected a well rated and respected diversified index, or what's called an ETF fund, from a trusted organization or management team with low expense ratios, you can set up monthly deposits scheduled to come from your specified bank account. This functions very similarly to your retirement contributions and just comes from your post-tax earnings. Be sure to speak to your financial advisor or institution to be sure you've set things up properly and you know how those savings are then invested in the selected investment fund of your choice.

GET PROFESSIONAL ADVICE

I do work with my financial advisor on my overall plan as well as my investments in the market. When I'm working on my real estate channel, I lean on my other team and keep my financial advisor updated. I've worked with different advisors in the past, some with the larger investment banks in the market. What can be frustrating is the overall cost, and how some of these firms tend to recommend their own products, likely due to incentives rather than due to looking at your overall individual plan and customizing it. That is why I recommend looking into a **fiduciary financial advisor**.

What is a fiduciary advisor? The legal term refers to an individual or organization responsible for acting on behalf of clients completely independently. They look to minimize any conflict of interests, which addresses some of the earlier concerns I've had and that you may have had in working with the brokerage firms. Fiduciary advisors are required to be registered with The Securities and Exchange Commission (SEC), which protects investors by regulating the markets in the USA. They typically have a background working in investment banks. To find one, you can contact the National Association of Personal Financial Advisors (NAPFA).

They are fee-based, and I do suggest meeting with a few of them to understand a bit more about how they operate and what services they provide, and then sharing with them your plan to see if it's a good potential partnership. You obviously do not need one to get started or need to have one as part of your team. However, they will have a different perspective on how to invest and how to help you reach your goals. You could, of course, manage all your investments yourself, but then it's all on you to make the right decisions. You want to be in a position where you already know the best assets even before you've come into those extra investment dollars to spend. And you want to minimize any time lost on errors in decision-making. Adding a fiduciary advisor can be critical to executing your net wealth plan effectively and efficiently.

I typically meet with my fiduciary advisor several times a year, and we go over my net wealth plan together. We have everything documented and work with my advisor's specialist tools and templates. I have my own financial net wealth plan. And we do some pressure testing, I share what I'm working on within real estate and other investments, and where I'd like to see things go with equities, and I share ideas on converting my IRAs to Roth IRAs as a possibility, etc. We might also share ideas on different lending opportunities, depending on where I'm at with my real estate portfolio. We also cover ideas on business structure and protection. It's been a great partnership, having someone who can challenge me and keep my plan in check. I highly recommend it as you start to build your second passive income channel in the market; as simple as it may seem, it's another valuable member of your team rooting for you to reach your goals.

And with that, you're almost there. Your first two passive income channels are building nicely and will ultimately become the majority asset creation vehicles that replace most of your earned income. We are going to explore a few more ideas, just to continue the themes of compounding and diversification strategies in adding different passive income channels to your asset mix.

But don't forget to cover the important to-dos. This channel needs to start as early as possible, where you may wait to purchase your first property. You want this channel humming along early to benefit from that compounding interest. And you just might want to double-check your retirement account allocation and contributions; it might be interesting to look at them again after your financial acumen has clicked up a notch.

READY, SET, GO!

Now, getting into the market will feel different from getting into real estate. It'll feel easier if you've already started investing in your retirement account (401K, IRA, or Roth IRA). What would be better is if your parents started a custodial Roth IRA when you were young and taught you the principles of compounding interest and diversification at an early age. But, unfortunately, most of us are learning as we go and doing our best.

If you haven't begun your retirement account, I would suggest you start there before you open an individual brokerage account. Look back at earlier steps in this book and be sure to take advantage of any employer incentives that go into a 401K, which is a great way to increase net wealth. Take the time to understand what has worked and what hasn't worked within your retirement account. Get to know the funds you've invested in and review their performance over the years compared to the broad index benchmarks.

Most importantly, look at the **expense ratios** of those funds. I keep harping on about this, but what exactly do I mean? What I am talking about is an annual fee expressed as a percentage of your investment. For example, if you invest in a mutual fund with a 1% expense ratio, you'll end up paying the fund $10 for every $1,000 invested. Or, in our example within this book, you'll end up paying $3,000 per year of a broad index fund that you will have built up to that $300,000 level. It may not seem like much per year, but you add those figures up year-over-year and eventually you'll look back and wish you had those funds to invest in other assets.

Now, I have no issue with paying someone a percentage from the return for great performance. And at times the brand name brokerage houses will promote how well their managers are doing. However, in my experience, there is little correlation between the level of fees to overall performance. I'm certainly not an expert but paying more for something that doesn't return something greater just doesn't make sense. Therefore, working with your fiduciary professional can help you. Remember: they are not working for an investment firm promoting their own assets; they have your plan in mind and want to maximize your returns while saving as much as possible in expenses.

Once you have your independent brokerage account set up, you're aligned with your fiduciary financial professional, and you have your index funds selected, you'll want to set up regular, monthly deposits into that account. These can be created by simply setting up automatic deposits by month on selected days from your preferred bank account. I suggest this approach, as this is what you are already doing with your retirement account. You're just using the extra income after taxes to make those deposits. This might be difficult in the early stages, when you're just getting started. Certainly, it will be challenging if you are living above your means, and you're not prepared to make those changes to free up extra money or to seek additional income to accelerate funds needed to start buying passive income assets.

Set this channel up early, as you want to benefit from principal build-up and compounding interest. While you are saving for your first real estate purchase, you should have your monthly contribution going. After you've invested and set up your regular contributions, you'll want to keep an eye on your market investments. Schedule regular touchpoints with your fiduciary advisor, but for the most part, your market investments will feel much more passive than your first passive income channel in real estate.

Why do both, buying real estate and investing in the market? This is a common question. There are pros and cons to each one, I have found. Investing in real estate requires more capital investment up front, some unique skill sets that you must build up over time with experience, and more work with capitalizing on opportunities and addressing challenges. The benefits, however, far outweigh the challenges. It's a terrific passive income investment and fits nicely in regular income payments to replace your earned income, plus the added benefits of appreciation and tax benefits really start to kick in more as you scale.

Investing in the market also has its pros and cons. It's much easier than with real estate to set up a compounding, diversified portfolio, and you can replicate a similar approach to your retirement account. Or you can mirror them both (if you haven't started yet on your retirement and wish to do both). It doesn't require as many people to be involved as real estate does, and just some basic research and tools will get you started. The cons are that so many things can pull the market up and down: geopolitical happenings, global pandemics, bubbles that burst, retail and Wall Street battles, and so on, that it would probably make you rather anxious if all you had were investments in the market.

That is why I suggest investing, learning, and growing in both channels. You'll work through the challenges of each, learn how to maximize the benefits, and develop ways of leaning on one over the other if things happen outside of your control. For example, if you have extended vacancies or repairs within your real estate portfolio that will take away from your passive income contribution, you'll have the market to cover you. Or, if there are unexpected losses in the market, you have that consistent, monthly passive cash flow coming in from your real estate.

It'll take a bit of a learning at the beginning, but you'll get the hang of it. Do this, and you'll have two passive income channels that will not only help you towards financial freedom but will also allow you to scale well past your initial plan. You'll need another plan after 10 years to grow even further if you wish to do so.

8

EIGHTH STEP: CROSSING THE FINISH LINE

Real estate investing is without doubt an incredible opportunity to build net wealth and passive income. It will also challenge you in lots of different ways. You're dealing with people who are part of an industry that may be different from the sector you work in, and they're looking to you for direction. There are banks and lenders that will challenge your plan and scrutinise every aspect of your financial interests such as property management, repairs, upkeep, marketing, tenants, liabilities, insurance, paperwork, you name it. Despite all this, the benefits of real estate far outweigh its challenges. At the end of the day, it is a passive income channel that will help you to replace half of your earned income.

On the flip slide, as your second passive income channel, the market is an incredible way to apply your diversification strategy and use time to allow your money to compound, building up a balance to eventually draw from and replacing almost a third of your earned income. It's much more hands-off than real estate, but it can have its curveballs, and many of these will be completely out of your control.

But it's good to find some other channels too, perhaps somewhere between those first two. And that's why I suggest you look at real estate syndication and reputable crowd-lending sources. These are alternative ways of building assets, net wealth, and passive income without some of the hassles of being a landlord or the risk from some of the broader market interruptions that will be outside your control. I wouldn't suggest they replace the top two channels, given their strength in passive income generation and scalability, but if you have the time and investment dollars within your plan, they may very well be the thing that help you cross the finish line and provide additional sources of passive income to support your overall vision.

REAL ESTATE SYNDICATION

So, if you're ready to test these out, let's look at a few ideas. The first additional passive income channel we should explore is this idea of real estate syndication. This is a bit more specialized than traditional buy-and-hold, and there are less syndication deals and investors out there. If you want to go down this road, you will have to be prepared to do your research and probably some networking to get an idea of what kinds of deals are available.

Real estate syndication is a way for investors to come together and collect their financial resources and invest in properties that they would not be able to purchase alone, given the size of the property and investment. They tend to be large commercial real estate properties, or they could be large apartment complexes, and they are usually in the multimillion-dollar price range. I'm not sure if they offer these types of opportunities outside of the USA, but you'll typically find these types of deals available all over the United States. To get started, you need to find a management company or sponsor of the property that has access to a pool of investors. Some of the reputable turnkey operators do these types of deals, as they have access to a large sponsor or management company and a set of investors that they can tap into. The management company will then acquire the property and manage its day-to-day operations.

As an investor, your role is to provide part of the equity toward the property. That's why, for me, it feels like an opportunity to combine the two previous passive income channels that we discussed into a hybrid. You're able to back into additional real estate asset wealth, without the headaches of being a full-time landlord, and you can flex your market acumen by investing in equity in a real estate asset. How it works: a sponsor will typically invest an initial amount in a property, sometimes 5% to 20%, then the investors put in the rest.

This is converted into passive income through property appreciation and rent. The rental income from a syndicate is distributed to investors from the sponsor of the property. It is typically transferred on a monthly or a quarterly basis. The property's value will, of course, appreciate over time, which will result in higher rents down the road, and higher earnings for investors, although you need to account for the costs of repairs and general upkeep.

One of the biggest advantages of syndication is that it is a lot less passive than managing your own real estate investment, and once investors receive their "preferred return," typically 10%, the remaining profits are split between the sponsor and the investors. But these deals aren't cheap, and usually the minimum investment is $50,000 or so. You are also placing a substantial sum of money into just one property, which is why I recommend that you spread your risk and have a mix of channels.

THE NITTY GRITTY

So far, this is all rather theoretical, so let's look now at a real example of a syndication deal I was working on early last year. This was a property that was built in the 1960s and had more than 100 units. Its purchase price, including the cost of repairs, was several million dollars. The numbers involved were too great for me to invest in alone, and the sponsor had a good reputation for management in the area and was putting up a sizable amount into the property to have some "skin in the game," which was a positive sign. They had also just completed a syndication within a similar size property in the same area with strong reviews from previous investors.

After accounting for the sponsor's acquisition, sourcing and management fees, investor estimates of profits were around a 9% "preferred return." A preferred return is a benchmark payment, distributed to all investors annually, of the money invested. So, for example, if I had $50,000 to invest, at a 9% preferred return, I could potentially take home $4,500 each year once the property earned enough money to make payouts possible. And for this example, that would happen after 2 years. Once each investor receives their preferred return, the remaining dollars are split between the sponsor and the investors based on the profit split structure. And in this case, it was a 50/50 split. What this means is that after everyone receives their preferred return in a 50/50 deal, and there is, say, $1M still remaining in profits, the investors would receive $500,000, and the sponsor would receive $500,000. The number of investors would determine the size of the allocation. As you can see, it's more passive than owning properties yourself, with potential cash flow and a good payout if the property is sold down the road, yet it's like owning a share of an asset, in this case, a property.

The challenge for me initially was finding reputable organizations offering real estate syndication deals with a proven history of delivering on their projections. But, once you do this, it's a great additional channel to add to your arsenal of net wealth building assets. I would encourage you to do more research. Bigger Pockets, an online real estate investment forum, is also a good source, as well as your local real estate investment communities.

TRY CROWD-LENDING

As an alternative to syndication, perhaps a little less complex but still new in the investment world, is the idea of crowd-lending. This is similar in concept to syndication, but for me, a bit easier to access. Essentially, it's an opportunity for "small-time" investors, perhaps like you and me, to fund larger projects. Or, if you are looking for more diversification, it's a way to spread your financial resources across a range of investments in projects around the country. I believe there are various crowd-sourcing opportunities out there for lots of different asset classes, but personally, I prefer those that are backed by real-estate. This is because it complements my knowledge as a real estate investor and is generally less volatile when compared to other classes, although it carries the risk of default and is not backed by traditional banking requirements and regulations.

Several of the types of assets available to invest in are either fix-flip (which is where you buy a property below market value, refurbish, and then sell it back to the market with increased margins), refinance, or purchase to rent investors looking outside of the traditional banking system for support for their initiatives (primarily due to how long it can sometimes take to acquire a loan). They are usually willing to pay higher rates of return to their investors, although minimal investments might be required, perhaps starting at $1,000. Typically, they have a portal to register, and you can login to review daily and weekly investment opportunities. Each one will include information on the terms of the loan (between 12 and 36 months), the maximum loan to value (from 50% to 80%, typically), and minimal yields and returns.

Additional information is provided about borrower details, such as the type of loan, the purpose and strategy of the project, credit history, payment terms, and where you fit as an investor, given a possible default on the loan. Returns are typically paid monthly, allowing you the opportunity to reinvest those earnings in other deals or withdraw for your passive income needs. I would strongly suggest you do your research on the platforms; a general search online is a good starting point. Read the reviews, ensure your platform of choice is transparent in its transactions, available states, interest payments, solvency, and overall, including how investments are collected in the event of default.

AN EXAMPLE

Let's take a quick look at a recent example. This was an opportunity available within one of the well-known crowd-lending organizations within the USA, which focuses exclusively on real estate-backed investment opportunities. An owner of a family residence in the southeast USA was seeking to refinance a home to fix and then to rent. It had 4 bedrooms, 2 bathrooms, and sat on 2,400 square feet**. The investment amount was more than $1M with an offering of the first lien position, which means that the crowd lending platform you use is the first entity to receive proceeds from a foreclosure if a loan is not repaid**. As an investor, this gives you added protection to recoup your initial investment.

On this deal, the details were appraised at $2M with 59% "loan-to-value," referring to the value of the loan relative to the estimated value of the property. The yield, or return offerings to you as an investor, were around 6.875%, for a term of 12 months. So, if you invested $5K at 6.875% over 12 months, you would have roughly $344 at the end of the loan. You might be asking, with mortgage rates so low, who would want to take these kinds of loans at a higher interest rate? These loans are for special situations such as rehabilitations and are not available through a conventional bank loan. It may not sound like much initially, compared to the proceeds from some of the other channels you are developing, but over time, as you spread out the number of loans for diversification and build up your portfolio within this channel, you can see how this will become a nice complement to your other passive income channels.

Also, during the current times, returns in these ranges are hard to come by given the fact that in the USA and much of the developed world, interest rates are historically low; but this may well change soon, when interest rates rise, offering an even greater opportunity for returns when financing is tougher to come by. This type of investment will carry some additional risk. For example, what if the individual defaults on their loan? This may happen occasionally, and your organization should have a clear process of how to collect what is owed. For those platforms that are backed by real assets, in this case properties, the asset is secured in a first-lien position, which places your investment first for repayment in a foreclosure situation. This will carry a bit more risk than the safety of secured investments, but those investments will have less of a return. That's the trade-off. But if you're moving and grooving as a real estate investor, picking up 1 or 2 properties in your portfolio and starting to get your feet wet, and you have begun to build an individual brokerage account that is compounding and well diversified, then I would encourage you to do some research and seek additional channels.

As you approach financial independence and look to transitioning from earned income to passive income, it's important to seek different channels to diversify your asset mix to help you achieve your net wealth objectives. There are others out there, such as REITs, or real estate investment trusts, which include purchasing shares or stocks in mutual funds and exchange-traded funds. These might feel more like market investing than real estate, but they are good to explore. Talk to your team, continue to network, but always keep in mind your net wealth plan. In the example in this book, you're looking for that additional 10% contribution to add to the existing channels that you are building up. That is, an additional 10% by the end of your 10-year plan (more or less, depending on your experience), but it supports your principles of compounding and diversification.

WORDS OF WARNING

If you have not yet completed your financial freedom journey, I want to take a moment to write down a few thoughts for you to consider, some "watch outs," if you will. The journey to gain financial freedom will not be easy. It will be achieved through your own personal sacrifices, as you go against the norms of constant spending. It'll come from delayed gratification, putting off that impulse to purchase while your family and friends post their latest travel adventure or treats on their social media feeds. It will come from giving up things and working on weekends and redirecting those precious extra earned income funds into asset-creating channels, which will ultimately provide you and your family the passive income streams to replace your earned income and to live a life on your own terms.

You will make mistakes, and there will be plenty of stress along the way. Anyone who has purchased real estate, invested in the market, or tried new investment ideas has a story of the ups and downs, and sometimes more downs than ups. That's okay. It's also a matter of perspective. If you have taken the steps to get your house in order and to increase the gap of your earned income today over your expenses, these mistakes will not impact you and your family's day-to-day life very much. You will have created those buffers to get through the early mistakes. So, mistakes are good, as they are a sign you are on your way. Here are a few "watch outs" that I'll share with you now, to help you cross that finish line:

Not all tax firms are the same. Early on, I would always do my own taxes. Even deeper into my career, my taxes never seemed that complicated. And I thought it was good for me to submit my own, to stay on top of the tax code per se. But then, I started increasing my earned income, and along with it came increases in my tax payments. My first firm came from a recommendation from a friend, and I found some peace of mind in having a group of professionals put my taxes together. But then, I started out on my net wealth building plan and quickly realized they did not have the type of expertise that I was looking for. There are several tax advantages of investing in real estate, and some considerations when building your portfolio while staying in your full-time job. Depreciation, payments on mortgage interest, property management, and repairs are all factors in owning real estate property. But you need a tax expert who understands how depreciation may impact you as an individual when approaching certain lenders. It's a balancing act, and you'll want to ensure you have the right advisors, those who understand what you are trying to accomplish.

Also, if you have more expenses than passive income, which may certainly be the case while you are in the early years of your plan, there are a set of rules to determine whether you can use those excess losses to offset other income from other sources, such as your salaried income. The general rule of thumb, today, is that if you make $100,000 or less each year, you can use up to $25,000 of excess rental losses to offset your other income. If your gross income is between $100,000 and $150,000, then you can only use part of your excess losses to offset your other income. But if you make more than $150,000 then you generally cannot use any of the excess real estate losses to offset income; however, you may carry them forward in future years.

That is why having a strong tax firm that specializes in people like you, who are building net wealth through real estate while maintaining other income, is essential. It's also important to understand how earned income is different from passive income, and how this can also be a good tax strategy for you in the future, when your portfolio is getting bigger, and a greater share of your income is coming from passive income.

Along with upgrading your tax team, there are also liability protections and business structures you'll want to become familiar with. **You need to protect your wealth**. Before building my net wealth and asset-creating channels, I really didn't think much about protecting my assets. Aside from perhaps a will, most of my previous assets were already accounted for. Any death benefits, retirement accounts, or simple ownership of personal assets didn't seem like something I should concern myself with by getting extra liability protections. However, when you start building your portfolio of real estate assets, brokerage accounts, and other channels, it's important to appreciate the additional risks to your newly acquired business and the appropriate protection you will need.

Take the time to interview and meet with several attorneys who can advise you on the type of structures you will need to achieve your vision. It's important to have your plan to share, given that they may recommend different types of structures based on the scaling of your plan. All businesses have liability risk, but when investing in real estate, there are additional pitfalls to be aware of. Someone may get injured at one of your properties, the house may burn down, and your reputation may be on the line if a tenant starts a lawsuit. You may not be thinking of these things today, but you will need to protect your assets now that you are coming into additional income and property. There are different levels of protection and legal entities to research so that you can determine which are best for you.

I suggest working with your new certified public accounting (CPA) firm and/or fiduciary advisor and getting them to advise you about firms that can help you to protect your newly acquired assets. Ask for several recommendations, be prepared to ask lots of questions, and really understand their strategies, how they approach each client and the costs associated with such a recommendation. I would not suggest picking the cheapest offering, I certainly did not. Go with the type of structure that works for your plan and invest in it while you are building. If you wait until you're almost at that finish line, there will likely be timing factors to work through when trying to pull it all together.

Not all financial advisors are the same. As you upgrade your tax and attorney team, I would suggest doing the same with your financial advisors. You may have never worked with an advisor before, and that's okay. If you already have someone who you are comfortable with and who knows where you are headed, keep going. But if you want someone specialized to look at those strategies within your retirement accounts, or the children's educational funds, or even regarding assessing your net wealth plan, I suggest finding a fiduciary financial advisor, either one in your area or one with a strong reputation who you'd like to connect with remotely.

As I mentioned previously, a fiduciary financial advisor is someone who acts on your personal interests and not those of an investment firm, which is often the case if you are working with an advisor who is tied to a brokerage firm. Nothing against those professionals; I have simply had better experiences with those who do not have those conflicts of interest. Take the time to determine what services you may need. If you are following these steps towards financial freedom, then you may want to consider looking into wealth planners, retirement planning, and estate planners to help you prepare your full estate. I would suggest you interview several, as not all fiduciary professionals are the same either. Look for someone you feel comfortable with, who understands your goals of financial freedom, and who has integrity. A good credential to also look for is "CFP", or certified financial planner, those who have met extra educational and experience requirements.

Be mindful of the expense; most fees average 1% per year, often on a sliding scale. This means that as your assets grow over time, the relative cost of your financial advisor should decline. To start your search, check out the National Association of Personal Financial Advisors (at napfa.org), which will allow you to find a financial advisor near you. You can also start to ask your team, and your friends or colleagues.

There are several other things to be aware of along the way, for each channel you set up, but the three listed in this section of the book will help ensure you are surrounded by highly qualified individuals who understand your plan and will help you execute it. Other things, such as researching any **medical insurance** you may need, or your specific tax implications, are also some "watch outs" I would suggest looking into. Several online groups of investors discuss these topics. Among others, you should examine during your net wealth building years. The important part is to reach out, network, build your team, and surround yourself with like-minded individuals. We can help each other address questions and provide support.

Keep these "watch outs" in mind as you progress toward your finish line, and let's quickly recap them here:

- Not all tax firms are equal.
- Protect your newly acquired asscts.
- Select an advisor carefully.
- Understand other implications such as medical insurance.
- Surround yourself with like-minded people.

ALMOST THERE

We're starting to get close to that finish line. And that might mean different things for you. You may be approaching completely replacing your earned income, yet still would like to continue to work in your full-time job for a while longer, this time with less pressure. It's certainly reassuring to have a Plan B. Or you may be crossing that finish line with the idea that you plan to retire early and replace your income with your new passive income channels. You might even decide to work part-time as a consultant or to take on a paid gig that is totally unrelated to your main career.

You might not want to stay in the same job, company, or industry for 40 years. It might be refreshing to try something new or make a switch, without sacrificing your current lifestyle or getting too concerned about how successful you might be in your new endeavor. We all know people who are jaded in their job yet are afraid to make a change given their current income or responsibilities.

You might also be closing in on that finish line just to take a step back from the rat race. You may want to travel, spend time with your family, or to step outside the whirlwind and be present for a bit. Let your mind and energy settle to perhaps gain some new perspective on life based on where you are on your journey. We don't all have to follow the same path of birth, school, working for 40 years, then, if you're lucky, retiring somewhere warm. I'm not actually sure if we are meant to live that way, but with so many people so unhappy under their exterior smile, the conventional route doesn't seem to be all it's cracked up to be, does it?

And early retirement or financial freedom is not about getting rid of everything and living as a minimalist. I realize there is a movement out there, but if that's not for you, that doesn't have to be your path. We've outlined a plan whereby you can maintain your current lifestyle, even grow with it over time, and still have your time back to do what you chose. And it's not about being lazy or just lounging around either. You'll have decades to build up more time and energy to put into the things that you are passionate about, so that when you do approach your retirement years, you already have your life rebalanced the way you've always wanted it. This might be the greatest gift you give yourself and your family.

As you approach the finish line, keep in mind the type of investor you want to be. This is not a book about getting rich quick or trampling over others to make a quick buck. This is about investing in real assets, growing wealth over time, and freeing up more time, perhaps in service to others and a greater good. As you build your real estate portfolio, think about the service you want your tenants to receive and the level of professionalism you expect your property management and other stakeholders to exhibit. When investing in the market, perhaps a more specific diversified asset allocation should go to those companies that are aligned with your values, and with the additional resources you now possess, you can start to flex your influence in choosing which to invest in to ensure those companies are successful.

When it comes to real estate syndication deals, you can choose to work with reputable syndication organizations or turnkey operators that are making a positive difference in their communities. For crowd-lending services, look for reputable platforms that are transparent, have solid business rules and practices in place, and secure positive projects to invest in. Look for companies that raise funds for communities and support local entrepreneurs.

There are plenty of opportunities out there to earn a return, but what does this all mean in the end? If you're caught up in the numbers, I would encourage you to revisit the earlier chapters of this book to remind yourself what it is all for. A greater tragedy would be to cross the finish line of financial freedom exhausted and to look around you and be unsure what to do with this gift.

Let's also make sure, when you cross that finish line, that you stay and even have a chance to reset a new line. You've likely heard of someone having some early success only to lose it in a risky investment, a litigation matter, or attempts at trying to time the market. You are in this for the long haul, building passive income streams that will forever replace your earned income for you and your family to enjoy financial freedom, and bringing forward your *Why* during your prime years when you are able to turn your dreams into a reality.

To cross that finish line, you'll want to be prepared for the roadblocks ahead. These may include certain tax strategies you'll want to consider in moving from earned income to passive income, enhanced legal structures (given the additional risk exposure you may be taking on with your passive income channel selection), and financial partners that have your best interest in mind and not that of an investment firm. I would suggest that once you have your plan together, you look at your current advisors, asking yourself if this the team that will help you cross that finish line and ensure you stay across despite the known and unknown obstacles ahead.

The journey itself will present so many ups and downs for you, but you'll find it rewarding in the lessons learned and even the type of person you will become. Crossing the finish line may or may not be met with the type of fireworks you dreamed of. I arrived in 2019, although I am still working in my full-time job, and I remember feeling more exhausted than elated, but I did take the time to look back at how far I had come. I taught myself everything I know, and I made so many mistakes along the way, but I have seen my sacrifices bloom into the fruits of my plan—and so can you.

I cannot wait for you to look at your accounts one day and suddenly see that you are taking in more passive income than earned income. It might be something only you get to see or to truly appreciate, but it will be well worth a celebration dance, even if you're sitting there in your pj's looking at the screen. Really take a moment. Put on that favorite song of yours and groove with it for a while. You deserve it.

EMBRACE MISTAKES

If you've arrived at this point, you'll have established yourself as a smart, well diversified investor, with cash flow and enough passive income assets to snowball into other investments. By following the steps in this book, you'll have taken some risks to build up a strong portfolio of asset classes. Sure, you might have made some mistakes along the way, but haven't we all? To be honest, I've made plenty. The first, from a financial point of view, was probably starting out as an actor (although from a more personal perspective, it's something I wouldn't change). It meant for the first 5 years of my career in biotechnology, I was effectively paying down debt rather than building up net worth. I had some real challenges with my initial foray into real estate investment, and when I started out with the market, I wasted money getting expensive advice that wasn't really a good value from brand-name investment houses rather than using a fiduciary advisor. The important thing to stress is that it's okay to make mistakes; it's necessary to learn and grow, if you don't let the setbacks derail you.

So, you have taken on some risk to build a strong portfolio of asset classes, you've made mistakes along the way in acquiring properties while investing in the market and learning what works and doesn't work in other channels. But you've crossed that finish line, and it should feel both exhilarating, terrifying, and exhausting. You did it! Your *Why* pushed you through the ups and downs, having your house in order protected you from the downs, and your commitment to compounding and diversification in different passive income channels built a foundation for you to replace your earned income and to achieve (in the words of the title) "financial freedom."

It moves me deeply to know that you have reached this place, as I know the sacrifices you've made, but think how much joy you will have in your heart as you are now able to execute your *Why*. We need more people like you, who are free from today's societal norms and comparisons and live life on their own terms. It's your time to come fully into yourself.

9

IT'S MORE THAN JUST NUMBERS

You have now either crossed the finish line or you have a very good picture of when and how this will happen. If you're not quite the left-brain person, your head might be spinning a bit. That's okay; hopefully the examples and anecdotes in this book have helped that right side of the brain connect to what we need to do with those numbers.

What I have written is intended to appeal to a different kind of people, those who are visual and those who learn through a step-by-step process. And it's constructed in a way that allows you to take a step at a time in logical order. It is a book of two halves, with the first half focused on your *Why* and getting your house in order, and the second a guide to executing your net wealth plan.

FULFILMENT

These steps, once achieved, will help you cross that financial independence finish line. But there is another finish line I want to talk about that doesn't have to do with the numbers. If you have received any sort of financial education, it was probably focused on saving, investing wisely, and figuring out what number you need to retire comfortably with. Through the steps in this book, I've shown you perhaps a different path towards independence, one that requires some different thinking and habits, but affords you the time and resources to spend your precious days as you like and not according to anyone else's agenda. What's missing in all of this is what to do with that extra time. Even if you make it to the retirement age of your mid-60s, you may be unsure of what to do with yourself.

Recent studies polled by the Nationwide Retirement Institute[5] showed that nearly 30% of recent retirees believed that life was worse in retirement than it was when they were working. Reasons for this included a sense of isolation and a loss of direction. For many of us, we've seen this phenomenon first-hand. How often have you heard from a relative that retirement just isn't all it's cracked up to be? And at the same time, many of our friends or family keep telling us we should be living every day as if it was our last—not easy to do when your trapped in the rat race of a 9-to-5 job. So, you know that all the money in the world won't bring you happiness, and that retirement alone might not bring you fulfilment. If this is the case, then why would anyone want to be financially independent anyway? Well, I feel fortunate that I woke up to the idea that retirement wasn't the main aim early on. There must be something else … perhaps another finish line we need to be aware of.

Some years ago, I was on a trip to the Congo, where I was working with a local non-profit that was supporting a group of students who aspired to be entrepreneurs. I was there to provide my two cents, but on these types of trips, I always take back more in lessons learned than advice that I can share. The Congo is one of the more challenging places to be in the world right now. And yet there is a real joy within the people and the culture, perhaps because living every day as if it were your last is something more of a reality. In this environment, I'm always reminded to enjoy the moment, to take a breath, and to find gratitude for the simple things in life.

But it was on my side trip to Tanzania that I realized how important it is to not only to plan for financial freedom, but to envision how you would want to spend your newly acquired time. It was the morning breakfast prior to our first safari trip, when I got chatting with a recently retired couple from the Midwest. They thought it was odd to find an American in his mid-30s, sitting alone, and reading a book on retirement. At first, they joked that I was a bit too young to worry about such things, but then I shared my aspirations to have more time on my hands to invest in the kind of things that I was passionate about.

They were curious about this and given that they were recently retired themselves, they were intrigued to learn what I was discovering. The book I was reading was *The New Retirementality: Planning Your Life and Living Your Dreams* by Mitch Anthony. In it, Mitch coins the term "return on life." As a financial advisor, he saw the gaps retirees were having around what was most important in life, and asked the question: what is the money for? This led to several questions I had for my new friends. Above all else, I wanted to know what life was like after recently retiring. And sure enough, they both wanted copies of the book, as they understood what Mitch was talking about. You see, the wife was a retired attorney who had argued in front of the Supreme Court of the United States, and the husband was a retired state judge who was used to having people stand up when he walked into a room. After retiring, all of that was essentially in the past. Or so they thought.

Part of the reason they were in Tanzania was to start working with an organization called Judges Without Borders, which is like Doctors Without Borders, whereby judges lend their expertise to developing nations dealing with a range of issues. And the issues he was working on (you could just see his energy perk up) were a range of human rights concerns in various countries around Africa, all of which he'd dealt with before in various capacities as a judge. The conviction he now had in discussing what he was doing, you could tell, was connected to his *Why*. He told me he wished he had come across this organization sooner, but his day-to-day couldn't afford him the time to think or even discover different ways to leverage his experience. That couple got involved in various similar projects, which allowed them to travel round the world and enjoy their sense of adventure, as well as give back to society within their retirement years.

This conversation around retirement has stuck with me during my entire financial freedom journey. It's reinforced how important it is, that as hard as you may be working on building your net wealth, you also must be working on your *Why* and how you plan to bring that vision to life. Don't wait till the end, as many do, to invest the time and energy during your journey to have the foundation set. Then when you are financially independent, you'll already know the kinds of things you want to shift your focus on with more time.

Now, there are a lot of resources out there to help you plan for this. I've personally read about 10 different books on these subjects and always take away a few things. One of my favorites is *How to Retire Happy, Wild, and Free* by Ernie J. Zelinski. It was written a while ago, and Zelinski has this positive tone, and his idea of starting the book on your last day of employment is an interesting one, as it really stresses the importance of starting with the end in mind. It's a great read, and I would really recommend it, even if you are still in your 20s or 30s.

LOOK FORWARD

In planning my own life, I have always broken it down into categories, and I assign certain goals to each of these areas. The various parts include spiritual development, health, family, friends, love, career, financial, adventure, and activities and items that may bring me and my family joy. I have found that I am at my peak happiness when I'm firing on most cylinders of these areas, and if I'm only firing on one or just a few, I'm not as happy. I don't think I've landed in a place where I've had them all firing at the same time; perhaps when I have more time I'll get there. But I'm always checking myself against those goals and looking for that right balance.

As part of that exercise and planning for more time in the future, I go through each category and see what percentage of time I am dedicating to each one. For example, I may be performing well at work by allocating more than 50% of my time there, but my family and friends may feel distanced, perhaps because when I think about my percentage of time with them, it is most certainly less than the time I spend at work. And sometimes this might be necessary to achieve your financial independence. But don't forget why you are doing what you are doing. If part of your *Why* behind financial independence is to have more time with your family and friends, you'll want to take steps to figure out what that looks like during your journey.

I like to go through each of these areas of my life and assign a current percentage of time allocation today. I then go through all these areas again to try and determine what life will be like after crossing that finish line. For example, if you're work is 50% and your family is less than 30% currently, perhaps you can switch these percentages once you are free, or perhaps spend even less time at work, given how you've defined it once financially independent. Your work might only draw only 10% of your time, given the successes you've achieved with your net wealth building plan containing assets that do not require you to live where your work is located, to commute, or to spend countless hours in meetings or transactions that take up most of your day. You will have the chance to spend more time with your family and friends and perhaps to allocate more time to the activities you enjoy, such as traveling.

But how well do you know your family and friends? What are those things that you enjoy doing together? If you live separately, what is the plan to live more closely together? How would you like to spend your time with them if you had more time? These are the questions you want to be working through, and not waiting until you've crossed that financial finish line.

It is my hope that you address these questions and strive for a life of true fulfilment, investing in the service of others and personally growing each day. You may need more time to educate yourself in some new skills, to network, and to discover organizations that align with your values, evaluating properties and land that are not in service of your portfolio, but are more philanthropic ideas, thinking through the organizations that you want to invest in with a mission that aligns with your *Why*. All these things are now possible with your extra time and resources. But spend the time now, go through those exercises, and envision the life you plan to have when you are financially independent.

You might want to stay at your regular job, just without all the stress and pressure. You may not need to chase the next promotion or job that takes you away from your family with more hours on the road or at the office. It may be taking some time away from the old job to decompress and take in life in a new light. The idea of having all the time in the world might seem like a dream for many, reaching back to the good old days of your youth, when you would spend your nights with your friends just hanging out.

Well, your 8 steps to financial freedom will create better days ahead. When you were younger with more time on your hands, you might not have had the wisdom or resources to know what to do with yourself; now you have both. The world needs more independent thinkers to reshape the way we do things. Too many of us are so caught up in the here and now, so that we simply don't have the time to think of what we would do if racing against the clock were no longer an issue. But that is the second finish line; let's be sure we cross it as well.

And be aware too that whilst you are on your journey towards financial freedom, your *Why* might change, I know mine has. I am on my second plan now, and it is my mission not only to replace my earned income but to create even further growth in the future. There are various reasons why I have decided to do this. First, I would like to contribute more to philanthropy, perhaps investing into healthcare in underdeveloped countries, and to be able to donate on a regular basis to several non-profits that are close to my heart. And on a more personal level, I want to travel more and to be able to help family and friends create their own financial goals.

MAKE A DIFFERENCE

If you've reached your goal of financial freedom, then congratulations. So many things had to line up for you to get to this point. You've probably had to overcome some setbacks and disappointments, and there might well have been some moments where you wondered if it was all worth it. However, your *Why* grounded you, and you might have even had a little luck along the way. But you did it: you've replaced your earned income with assets that will generate passive income year-over-year for you to free more time to invest as you choose. You no longer need that full-time job because you've set yourself up for financial independence. It's an incredible achievement, and it brings with it great responsibility. You are now completely free to do the things you've always wanted to do, with the opportunity to fully come into who you are, and you've got time and years ahead to accelerate into those next chapters. The responsibility I believe we investors have is to bring integrity, respect, and an appreciation of the needs of others to our dealings.

It's up to you now, as we need leaders to redefine the rules. So many industries seem to be out of touch with what is happening in this world, and this means that the people who work in them also tend to work towards goals or incentives that are outdated or not really aligned to what we need right now.

I'm not so far in the clouds to think that one person can fix all this. But I do think that a group of people who have taken the steps reflected in this book are in a good position to have the kind of influence and perspective this world needs, at the local, national, and international level.

Have the courage to flex your *Why* and to use your new time and resources to inspire a different way of thinking.

KEEP MOVING

Whatever you do, don't stand still. My grandfather's favorite quote was, "We gotta keep movin'." He died when he was 96 after really making something of himself, despite the fact he didn't start with much, apart from a lot of ambition and courage. He was born in a small town in Texas during the Great Depression, and he became a Purple Heart veteran during WW2, when he was injured parachuting behind enemy lines on D-Day. After meeting my grandmother after the war, he was happily married for 73 years. Neither of them had much except their strong hearts and hopes for a better future.

My grandfather was a natural salesman, and in his 40s, when he became tired of managers telling him how to do things and placing a price tag on his time, he set up his own packaging business, which became a small regional boxing corporation. He no doubt had his challenges in running his business, but his previous experience and determination to have a better life meant that challenges would not hold him back. He later retired and sold the business to one of the international packaging corporations. He spent the later years of his life happily tending the farm where he lived with my grandmother, which was a great place to raise horses and cattle. He was fully into his own joy by then, you could tell. My grandfather taught me so many things about life, and his greatest advice to me was to "just keep movin'." He would say that if you stop, that's when things run into trouble in your life. "Even when you think you've made it", he would go on, "it's up to you to help others keep on moving by your example."

It's simple advice, but it has always stuck with me. You see, financial freedom is not a journey to take towards ending in some sort of early retirement state so you can lay around and do nothing without a care in the world. Perhaps you may need a break for a bit, but you'll soon realize that this kind of life is not really what you wanted. Instead, by earning the right to be free, you can move into your *Why.* Take charge of your life, make things happen, and don't let anyone take away your dreams. Stay close to those who matter, and don't put too much stock in what others think. You're talented, gifted, smart, and strong, so get after it.

I guess you could say that some of my grandfather's advice is wrapped up in this book. So, let's keep moving. Make that next 5- or 10-year plan, all while enjoying your new freedom. What is possible now that you've crossed that finish line? Is there more to your *Why* than you first thought? Could crossing that initial finish line help you to discover new challenges around the corner, challenges that you never dreamed of taking on?

You've successfully set up passive income channels that can provide for you and your family in perpetuity. You could stop and live off the cash flow coming in for a while or start focusing straightaway on the purpose of life and the extra time you have. Either way, keep going. Keep moving. If you need to reset your goals and think bigger, I suggest extending your network to those who can push you. Perhaps you want to double your passive income streams to create an even better lifestyle for you and your family or to have greater security. Perhaps you want to try different jobs or reset a new career given the time that you now have. The world looks different when you are in your 40s compared to your early 20s, when you were supposed to know what you wanted to do for a career. Maybe you just want to take that extra time to start the non-profit you've always dreamed about. Now, you have that chance. Maybe you've wanted to donate to your select charities, invest in their boards, or to provide your experience and vision.

Perhaps you've wanted to teach, coach, and give back to your community. Just because you're financially independent and have your next chapter successfully lined up doesn't mean your life just stops or pauses. In fact, if you've done it right, your life has taken a whole new turn. Share your successes, your lessons learned, and create a community of investors who are equally committed to using their resources in the service of others. Just keep moving, as my grandfather would say. It's now your time to step into this next chapter with the time, resources, and influence to perhaps reshape the way things are done in this world. However big or small is up to you. You just need to keep moving …

10

SEE YOU AT THE FINISH LINE

Thank you for coming along with me on this journey, which I hope has inspired you to think through where you are today, where you want to be, and the steps you may need to take to get there. My hope is that you take action on these steps to gain your desired financial freedom, to truly come into who you are and into your sense of purpose. Life can get a bit crazed at times; it can sometimes disappoint us, as we think it was supposed to turn out differently, given the path that was shown to us. I hope the contents and roadmap of this book inspire you to reconnect with your dreams and aspirations no matter where you are in your journey, what previous path you took, or what challenges you face. Take that first step, and I'll **see you at the finish line**!

NOTES

1. U.S. personal saving rate monthly 2020. https://www.statista.com/statistics/246268/personal-savings-rate-in-the-united-states-by-month/#
2. Taxing-wages-united-states pdf (oecd.org). http://www.oecd.org/tax/tax-policy/taxing-wages-united-states.pdf
3. Nominal Wage Tracker | Economic Policy Institute (epi.org). https://www.epi.org/nominal-wage-tracker/#
4. American Household Credit Card Debt Statistics: 2020 NerdWallet. https://www.nerdwallet.com/blog/average-credit-card-debt-household/
5. Many Americans Appear to Have a Discouraged Outlook on Retirement, But There's Hope (nationwide.com). https://news.nationwide.com/many-americans-appear-to-have-a-discouraged-outlook-on-retirement-but-theres-hope/

Acknowledgments

Writing this book has been an incredible journey, especially during these crazy times. The lessons I have learned would not have been possible without my late grandpa Jim and my father John. These two men had the most influence on my life, both in business and in service of others. My inspiration and drive derive from my late grandmother Polly and my mother Linda. Collectively, these two women showed me strength and grace.

My heroes today are my siblings, my brother Jon and my sister Kristy. Based on the cards we were dealt at such an early stage in life, it is incredible to see how we have persevered. Their love and support continue to give me the courage to set new standards of what it is I can do. I also want to thank my girlfriend Vina, Auntie, her two girls, and our Pomeranian Foxy for supporting me during the writing of this book, during a time in life that was unlike any other. And thank you to my close friends Joel, Wilmar, and Ankur for helping me formulate this idea of financial freedom.

Thank you to all those who have been part of this journey with me: Candice and Larry with my initial real estate; Ryan and the team at Creative Planning; Michele and Brandon for all the legal and tax advice; Alex, Andrew, and Joe with scaling real estate; and the team at Peer Street. You have helped me formulate these steps that have not only provided a path towards freedom and greater possibilities, but also have afforded me the opportunity to gain the experience I would need to draw from in the examples expressed in this book.

A special thanks to all my colleagues within the biopharmaceutical, academic, and creative arts industries. It has been a challenging time for everyone, but also a time in which we have been able to showcase some incredible innovation, science, and new ways of helping individuals around the globe. Thank you for taking the time to help me develop the skills and acumen that I can apply to the job and to initiatives such as this. The opportunities you have afforded me over the years have brought me into the professional I am, and I am eternally grateful.

Finally, thanks to my incredible editors Lucy Benyon and Laura Pasquale for being so patient with me and helping me pull this book together, and for the incredible work by my creative designer Steve Kuhn and associate Michael Doane for assisting in bringing this concept to life. Your support and encouragement have brought me to the finish line!

About The Author

James B. Keefe is the author of 8 Steps to Financial Freedom: Achieve Independence Earlier and Live Life on Your Own Terms. A working professional by day and an investor in new ideas, he received his MBA in Global Management from Thunderbird Graduate School of Global Management and his BBA from the University of Wisconsin-Madison. He has coached for Special Olympics for the past 12 years as well as mentored with Big Brothers Big Sisters and the Philadelphia Futures organizations. A globe trotter with 84+ countries and counting, you may find James on land Latin dancing or down below ocean diving while working on his underwater photography.

Connect with James B. Keefe on
www.linkedin.com
to continue the conversation.

www.ingramcontent.com/pod-product-compliance
Ingram Content Group UK Ltd.
Pitfield, Milton Keynes, MK11 3LW, UK
UKHW022003190726
13853UKWH00004B/1709